TRAINS

A MISCELLANY

RAY HAMILTON

summersdale

TRAINS

Copyright © Summersdale Publishers Ltd, 2015

Illustrations © Shutterstock

All rights reserved.

No part of this book may be reproduced by any means, nor transmitted, nor translated into a machine language, without the written permission of the publishers.

Ray Hamilton has asserted his right to be identified as the author of this work in accordance with sections 77 and 78 of the Copyright, Designs and Patents Act 1988.

Condition of Sale
This book is sold subject to the condition that it shall not, by way of trade or otherwise, be lent, re-sold, hired out or otherwise circulated in any form of binding or cover other than that in which it is published and without a similar condition including this condition being imposed on the subsequent purchaser.

Summersdale Publishers Ltd
46 West Street
Chichester
West Sussex
PO19 1RP
UK

www.summersdale.com

Printed and bound in the Czech Republic

ISBN: 978-1-84953-709-4

Substantial discounts on bulk quantities of Summersdale books are available to corporations, professional associations and other organisations. For details contact Nicky Douglas by telephone: +44 (0) 1243 756902, fax: +44 (0) 1243 786300 or email: nicky@summersdale.com.

For Mum, who can still remember the old steam train that ran along the line between Gryffe Crescent and Morar Drive, and the trouble her boys got into later playing on the disused line!

ACKNOWLEDGEMENTS

My thanks yet again to all at Summersdale Publishers (IPG Trade Publisher of the Year 2014!) for the opportunity and support to write another book on a subject of huge interest to me. On this occasion, I am particularly grateful to Claire Plimmer for the opportunity, Sophie Martin for steering the project through to completion, and Abbie Headon for her superb editorial input. My thanks also to Julian Beecroft for his thoroughly helpful copy-edit.

CONTENTS

Foreword..6

Introduction...8

Getting History on Track.......................12

Riding the Railways of the World........64

Some of the Great Trains.....................95

Iconic Railway Stations.......................124

Great Railway Journeys.......................149

Across Cities, Mountains and Seas....172

Trains on Film......................................194

Trains in the Arts.................................210

Railway Preservation and Enthusiasm...............247

Full Steam Ahead................................270

FOREWORD

Even in the twenty-first century, rail travel fascinates actual and would-be travellers, and there's still a whiff of romance and adventure about it too – certainly for intrepid passengers on the 13:50 to Vladivostok, if not for commuters on a delayed 17:23 to Peckham. It has always fascinated me, and it was a love of trains and travel which led to my first solo overseas trip at the tender age of 13, to the exasperation of my parents – even if that was merely a day return from London to the Isle of Wight. It led me to join British Rail as a graduate entrant, where I saw rail operations at the sharp end as Station Manager for Charing Cross and London Bridge, and later experienced the political angle working at the Department for Transport. In 2007 I gave up the day job to concentrate on what started as a hobby but which is now my full-time occupation: running the train travel website 'The Man in Seat 61', helping people take the train in Europe and worldwide, and so recapture that sense of adventure and romance away from soulless flights or dreary motorways. So if there's anyone who feels the lure of the rails, it's me!

When you start reading *Trains: A Miscellany*, you'll doubtless feel it too – if you don't already, of course. Ray Hamilton takes you on a breathtaking canter across this whole intriguing subject, sketching the highlights (and sometimes lowlights) of railways and train travel across 150 years of operation and dozens of countries worldwide, from famous trains and iconic stations to historical anecdotes and classic railway quotes.

It's a journey in itself – an ideal read the next time you settle into a comfortable window seat, hear the brakes gently hiss off, and listen for that clickety-clack to start...

Mark Smith
The Man in Seat 61
(www.seat61.com)

INTRODUCTION

The introduction of so powerful an agent as steam to a carriage on wheels will make a great change in the situation of man.

Thomas Jefferson, 1802

We all remember the excitement of first seeing trains as children, and many of us were lucky enough to have train sets of our own, whether the wooden ones that have to be pushed around the track or the more sophisticated ones that seemingly travel on metal rails of their own accord, sounding and looking for all the world like the real thing. Trains also cropped up frequently in our children's books and TV programmes. Not knowing as a child who Thomas the Tank Engine is compares with not knowing that ice cream exists as a foodstuff. Sooner or later comes the exhilaration of getting on an actual train and chattering excitedly about everything that could be seen from the window. ('Look, a sheep!')

But then something even more amazing happens. In the years that follow, we discover that the joy and excitement of travelling by train doesn't disappear after we have tired of squealing at the sight of a sheep, cow or car. We discover the possibilities of rail travel and the destinations on offer to us. Other towns and cities in our own country suddenly don't seem nearly so far away, and nothing can be more foreign than the first train journey we experience in a different country altogether. The shapes and colours of the trains are different abroad, and the sights, sounds and smells of the journey are ones we have never before experienced. 'This is the life,' we think. And it is.

In my early twenties I 'did Europe' on an InterRail pass with a friend. We had planned to take in as many countries as possible in a month but loitered too long on the French Riviera before travelling the length of Italy. So we managed only two countries (or four if you include the principalities of Monaco and San Marino), but we absorbed them in a way that would not be possible travelling by any other means. The combination of carefree journeys and anticipated destinations offered by rail travel has always been hard to beat.

I have been lucky enough since then to travel further afield by rail, including a journey on the overnight sleeper from Jaisalmer in Rajasthan's Thar Desert to New Delhi (when Indian families without two rupees to rub together insisted on sharing their home-cooked pakoras and bhajis with my wife and me), a tiffin lunch on the heritage British-built North Borneo Railway (on which pith-helmeted waiters only ever stopped smiling for the more serious business of having their photographs taken with us), and a trip from Adelaide to Melbourne on Australia's Great Southern Rail. In Mumbai we jumped on to local trains for a couple of stops just to experience the colourful sea of saris and happy, smiling faces that could not have contrasted more with those of glum, grey commuters into London if they tried.

I have dipped into the past on a number of other heritage railways, such as the vintage diesel Conway Scenic Railroad in New Hampshire, the Strathspey Steam Railway in the Scottish Highlands and the Golden Arrow Pullman experience of the Bluebell Railway in Sussex, and I have ridden the bang-up-to-date present on the Skytrains of Bangkok and Kuala Lumpur. The fact is, you have to travel to some pretty remote places to be far from an opportunity to jump on your next train.

Whether you yearn for the romantic age of the steam engine, thrill at the speeds reached by today's superfast trains, dream of travelling on the world's great long-distance rail journeys, or yearn to take the narrow-gauge 'Toy Train' up to the tea plantations of Darjeeling, this book offers you a whistle-stop tour of all that is fun and interesting about the intriguing story and ongoing excitement of train travel.

So hop on board, sit back and enjoy the ride!

GETTING HISTORY ON TRACK

The time will come when people will travel in stages moved by steam engines, from one city to another, almost as fast as birds fly, 15 or 20 miles in an hour.

Oliver Evans, 1812

While the genius of British inventors and engineers may have kick-started the Industrial Revolution in the nineteenth century, their American counterparts were not exactly slouching around either. Oliver Evans was one such genius on the other side of 'the pond', and he was spot on when he prophesied that steam-powered engines would one day travel as fast as 20 mph, though he understandably failed to foresee the further advances that would allow people to travel on futuristic trains at over 250 mph in our own century. This chapter provides a potted history of the pioneers and events that have brought us to a time when we can gallop across whole countries on trains that levitate at bewildering speed over electromagnetic tracks. Oliver Evans may have been somewhat surprised to see us doing so without so much as holding on to our hats.

PRE-LOCOMOTIVE TIMES

 There are records dating back to around 600 BC of wheeled vehicles being pulled by humans and/or animals along rudimentary tracks for the purpose of transporting goods or even to haul large boats across land from one body of water to another. It would take another 2,400 years for mankind to figure out how to harness steam to generate locomotion, but in the meantime they devised other methods of transportation, most notably the horse and carriage combination and widespread networks of canals.

Industry also experimented with and improved upon the rail systems they used to haul goods by hand or horse, so wooden rails had been replaced with iron ones, and flanges (either on the rails or on the carriage wheels) prevented the carriages from leaving the tracks.

By 1775, however, Scottish inventor James Watt had created a steam-powered mechanical engine that could turn a wheel, and the writing was on the wall for horses and barges alike.

STEAMING AHEAD IN THE NINETEENTH CENTURY

By the turn of the nineteenth century, the Industrial Revolution was in full flow and there was a pressing demand for a better and faster way to move manufactured goods around. Britain, as we shall see, was soon leading the way with a solution, but the rest of the world (and the USA in particular) wouldn't be far behind:

1804: The world's first self-powered railway journey took place when Cornishman Richard Trevithick built the first steam locomotive and used it to haul carriages at Penydarren iron works in Wales at 5 mph. It proved too heavy to be of practical use.

1812: Englishman Matthew Murray built the steam locomotive *Salamanca* and ran it successfully to haul coal along the narrow-gauge, rack-and-pinion Middleton Railway in West Yorkshire. The railway had been built in 1758 for horse-drawn carriages and remains the world's oldest operational heritage railway to this day.

1813: The *Puffing Billy*, built by William Hedley, was used to haul coal wagons by steam and friction along regular rails in Northumberland, England. It proved so reliable that it continued in use for a staggering 50 years. The oldest locomotive still in existence, it remains a magnificent sight at the Science Museum in London.

1825: The Stockton and Darlington Railway was opened in north-east England to transport coal, enabled by wrought-iron track (which was much stronger than the cast iron previously used) and hauled by locomotives engineered by Englishman George Stephenson and his son Robert, including the famous *Locomotion No. 1*, which remains preserved at the Darlington Railway Centre and Museum.

1829: Robert Stephenson's *Rocket*, which had evolved from *Locomotion No. 1*, won the locomotive trials that were held at Rainhill near Liverpool to find the locomotive best suited to operate on the under-construction Liverpool to Manchester Railway. The victorious *Rocket* became the template for most steam engines for the next 150 years.

1830: The first regular passenger service in Britain commenced upon George Stephenson's completion of the Liverpool to Manchester Railway, the same year that the pioneering Baltimore and Ohio Railroad carried its first passengers in the USA.

MR TURNER AND
MR STEPHENSON

In many ways, George Stephenson was the J. M. W. Turner of the engineering world. As contemporary geniuses born on the wrong side of the tracks, they each had to overcome the ridicule of their respective establishments to make their way in the world. Turner fought the art establishment and won. Stephenson, an illiterate self-educated maverick from Newcastle upon Tyne, was initially laughed out of the House of Commons after trying to persuade Members about the merits of his hare-brained railway schemes. After he started to conquer valleys, rivers and peat bogs with his engineering prowess, however, they stopped laughing and started investing.

TRAGIC START

At the gala opening of the Liverpool to Manchester Railway in 1830, William Huskisson, the Member of Parliament for Liverpool, stepped down from his train to go and speak to the Duke of Wellington, only to fall onto the adjacent track just in time to be run over by Robert Stephenson's *Rocket*. He bled to death from his injuries.

1832: English civil engineer Charles Fox, who went on to become a stalwart of George Stephenson's railway-building empire, invented the railway switch, or points, which allowed trains to run freely when diverting from one track to another.

EARLY EXAMPLES OF SIDERODROMOPHOBIA

Siderodromophobia is the medical term for a fear of trains, from the Greek *sidero* (iron), *dromo* (racecourse) and *phobia* (fear). But that condition is surely nothing compared with the fear of the unknown that many people felt when the first iron monsters appeared in the nineteenth century. Here are some of the most common fears that prevailed during the early years:

➤ As it won't be possible to breathe travelling at 30 mph or more, it is bound to result in collapsed lungs and ribcages.

➤ The human eye will be damaged having to adjust to such constant motion.

➤ Cows grazing in fields near passing trains will produce stale milk.

➤ The smoke will blacken the fleeces of sheep.

➤ Poor people from the country will travel on trains to the cities and pick rich people's pockets when they get there.

1833: The English engineering genius Isambard Kingdom Brunel was appointed chief engineer of the Great Western Railway (GWR) at the age of just 27. Within eight years the line from London to Bristol would become one of the wonders of the world, incorporating numerous engineering firsts, and Brunel would go on to revolutionise the infrastructure of travel around the world.

1834: The Dublin and Kingston Railway was inaugurated in Ireland, and is widely believed to have provided the first dedicated commuter service in the world, because its primary purpose was to transport men between their homes in Dublin and their workplace at the docks. It was built by the indomitable William Dargan, Ireland's answer to Brunel, and now forms part of the Dublin Area Rapid Transit (DART) system.

1835: Belgium led the way in Continental Europe when it opened a commercial railway from Brussels to Mechelen. Germany's first commercial railway was opened in Bavaria later that same year, running from Nuremberg to Fürth.

RIP THEIR FLESH OFF!

They took rail-passenger behaviour seriously in nineteenth-century Ireland, with jail sentences handed out for even minor offences. One 9-year-old child was sent to jail for annoying other passengers while playing with some marbles. If that scale of justice were to be applied to present-day rail travel, passengers who scream into mobile phones with their mouths full of half-chewed burger would presumably be sentenced to have their flesh ripped off by rabid dogs. Just saying.

HOW DOES THIS THING WORK?

Germany's first locomotive, *Der Adler* (*The Eagle*), was delivered in 1835 from the Robert Stephenson locomotive works in Newcastle upon Tyne complete with a driver, because Germany didn't yet have a driver of its own. This was true of many of the early locomotives exported from Britain. If you didn't have any trains, you couldn't learn to drive them!

1836: London's first railway station opened at London Bridge.

1839: George Bradshaw's publishing company in Manchester produced the first ever compilation of railway timetables. The timetables and associated travel guides that bore his name would become the rail traveller's bible and remain in print until 1961.

1840: The Great Western Railway adopted 'London Time' (GMT) across its network (Bristol, for example, was in fact 14 minutes behind London at the time), to help people avoid missing trains and to reduce the likelihood of accidents caused by the different timetables in use around the country. A standard railway time was soon adopted throughout Britain and the rest of the world gradually followed suit.

1843: Queen Victoria made the first of her many train journeys. The railways allowed her to meet a lot more of her subjects and more easily to visit her favourite residences at Balmoral in the Scottish Highlands and Osborne House on the Isle of Wight.

DEAD CHEAP RAIL TRAVEL

The legal and illegal bodysnatching trades received a bit of a boost upon the arrival of the railways, as getting bodies to medical schools and university hospitals was a much quicker procedure by train, and cadavers were therefore much fresher. In Victorian Britain, it was perfectly legal to buy dead paupers from alehouses, dead lunatics from asylums, and executed murderers from the state, before loading the day's haul into the 'dead carriage' at the back of the train. So-called resurrectionists practised a less legal trade, digging up bodies within hours of them being buried, hence the derivation of the term 'holding a wake', coined by mourning relatives as they sat by their loved one's grave until the loved one in question was stale enough to be automatically refused a train ticket.

I LOVES A GOOD MURDER, I DOES!

In Victorian Britain, people had an insatiable appetite for the macabre, often travelling long distances by train to visit the site of a particularly gruesome murder. When railway companies started to run special excursions so that they could also witness the ensuing public hanging, tickets sold like hot cakes. Executions were often arranged on market days, so that those visiting the town by train would be able to fit in a bit of shopping on the way back from the hanging to the railway station.

1844: Lower-class travellers in Britain were originally priced as, and pretty much treated as, freight. The 'Gladstone Act' of 1844 required that third- and fourth-class carriages should at least be covered so that passengers were not showered in hot coals during the journey.

1846: The first Crampton locomotives were built with low-slung boilers and huge driving wheels, based on the design of English engineer Thomas Russell Crampton, and reached speeds of 75 mph.

PRENDRE LE CRAMPTON

Crampton locomotives proved so popular in France that the term *prendre le Crampton* remained synonymous with catching an express train long after the locomotives themselves had disappeared from service. One of the original locomotives has been preserved in the Cité du Train, the world's largest railway museum, at Mulhouse.

1848: William Henry Smith opened the first railway bookstall and news stand at London Euston Station. WHSmith stores grace many railway stations to this day.

RAILWAY MANIA

Following the commercial success of the Liverpool to Manchester Railway and the Baltimore and Ohio Railroad in 1830, there followed a mad rush to make fortunes from the 'rapid' transportation of people and freight. In the decades that followed, locomotive design improved exponentially through the trial and error of different components and wheel arrangements. Tracks were laid like mad around Britain, Europe, America and, not surprisingly, throughout the British Empire. Such a fast-growing worldwide network must have been akin to a solid World Wide Web for the Industrial Revolution, changing the world forever in a short space of time.

We are all told nowadays that travel broadens the mind as well as the horizon, but imagine living through a time when millions of people around the world got to see the sea for the first time in their lives. It must have been all they talked about when they returned to their homes and workplaces. Here are just a few of the other momentous changes that took place in the middle of the nineteenth century:

➤ Towns and cities grew like Topsy, as entire rural communities arrived by train in search of work.

➤ Goods could be transported to markets and to ports with unprecedented speed.

➤ Newspapers and mail could be read across the land on the day of publication or composition, and international news not much later. Communication was here to stay.

➤ Holidays at the seaside or in the country, or even abroad, became a reality for millions of people. As well as being exciting, this was also hugely educational if you'd never been further than your feet or horse could carry you.

➤ Shopping expeditions could be made to towns and cities, and you could easily get your purchases home that same day.

➤ The arts became accessible to millions of people for the first time, as museums, art galleries and theatres became suddenly reachable as a day trip.

➤ Women became less reliant on men to travel just about anywhere (even if, in Victorian Britain, guidebooks felt the need to advise women to place pins in their mouths to avoid unwanted kisses when going through railway tunnels).

➤ Countries were able to establish closer national identities by bringing together the often disparate states and communities that had existed hitherto.

➤ Sport finally reached the masses. Football, rugby and cricket leagues grew as teams and supporters travelled by train to away matches, sporting heroes turned up to play in the provinces, and railway stations were built alongside sporting venues like racecourses and golf courses.

Even those who didn't travel much on the trains of the nineteenth century would have been grateful for them and/or fascinated by them. Trains brought business that would never have otherwise materialised, and those who got rich quick included hoteliers, newspaper publishers, postcard and souvenir makers, and English hop growers, not least because railway workers were paid partially in beer. Trains were often purpose-built to carry specific goods, and here are just a few of the products that trains allowed many people to see for the first time in their lives:

1. Bananas
2. Fresh fish and seafood
3. Racehorses
4. Building materials
5. Local delicacies
6. The luggage of the upper classes

1. These were ripened on the move with steam pumped from the locomotive.

2. The sight and smell would have been a new experience to the millions who had never been to a seaside. The advent of the railways created the modern trawling industry and made fish affordable.

3. These could now be delivered straight to racecourses, whereas previously horses could only race in their local area.

4. These were for the construction of houses, hotels, factories and ships.

5. Many of these became global phenomena once they could be transported to seaports and beyond. They included foodstuffs as diverse as haggis, Eccles cakes, Pontefract liquorice and Cornish pasties from the British Isles, the inhabitants of which were able to sample exotic foreign foodstuffs in return.

6. The well-to-do travelled with vast amounts of clothing and equipment and servants to allow them the best possible preparation for the Scottish grouse moor, the Mediterranean bathing resort or the Alpine ski slope to which they were heading.

1851: The line between Moscow and St Petersburg was completed in Tsarist Russia.

1852: The British Raj opened its first stretch of railway in India, inaugurating the Great Indian Peninsula Railway with 25 miles of track from Bombay (now Mumbai) to Thana (now Thane) in the state of Maharashtra.

1853: The world's first 'union station' (so-called because more than one railway company operates from it) opened in Indianapolis, Indiana.

1860s: The advent of more durable and comparatively inexpensive steel allowed the transition from wrought-iron railway tracks, resulting in a further boom to the networks being built around the world.

1863: The world's first underground railway was opened to get commuters from London Paddington to Farringdon Street (for the Bank of England) without having to inhale the smog and manure that permeated the air of the horse-drawn rush hour above. However, as the underground trains were pulled by steam locomotives, the smoke-filled tunnels they travelled in probably weren't much better for their health.

1863: The world's first steam-driven, narrow-gauge railway was opened in Snowdonia in north Wales.

GAUGING THE PROBLEM

Narrow-gauge railways, cheaper to build and better suited to the tight twists and turns of industrial areas and mountainous terrain, went on to run industry worldwide for a hundred years. Standard gauge, which George Stephenson had set at an imperial 4 foot 8.5 inches (1.435 m), was more suited to fast, level track, but not all railway companies fell into line with the Stephenson standard and many developed their own 'standards' instead.

The Regulating the Gauge of Railways Act was passed in 1864 in Britain to end the 'gauge wars' and sort out the mess caused by the incompatibility of 'standard' gauges used by trains around the country. The Great Western Railway, however, remained a law unto itself on Brunel's broad gauge of 5 feet and a quarter of an inch (2.14 m) and did not fully convert to Stephenson's standard gauge until 1892. Today, over 60 per cent of the world's rail networks, and almost all of its high-speed track, operate on Stephenson's standard gauge. Broader gauges remain prevalent on the Indian subcontinent and throughout eastern Europe.

1861–65: The American Civil War was the first major conflict in which the train played a significant part, as troops and equipment could be moved to battlefronts with unprecedented speed.

1866: The bubble burst on overvalued railway stocks and shares, the most important and popular investment on the London Stock Exchange at the time. The Brontë sisters were among the many investors who lost out.

1869: In the USA, the Union Pacific and Central Pacific railroad tracks finally joined up in Utah, thereby reducing coast-to-coast travelling times from 6 months to 7 days.

CHINA AND IRELAND JOIN FORCES IN UTAH

On 10 May 1869 in Promontory Summit, Utah, the huge, predominantly Chinese workforce of the Union Pacific railroad company finally met the huge predominantly Irish workforce of the Union Pacific railroad company coming the other way. Together they had battled tough working conditions and extreme weather conditions for six long years to unite the two coasts of the country to which they had emigrated from quite opposite directions.

1870: The word 'weekend' first appeared in the Oxford Dictionary after towns like Hastings, Ramsgate and Eastbourne on England's south coast had started to offer an early Monday morning service back to London, thereby opening up the possibility for city workers to enjoy a new phenomenon: a 'weekend' at the seaside.

1872: American inventor George Westinghouse patented his first automatic air brake, which remains the basis of modern-day train-braking systems.

1879: The first practical electric railway was produced by Werner von Siemens in Germany, paving the way for countless metropolitan rail systems around the world (steam locomotives were never suitable for use within built-up cities). It was the first train to pick up electricity as it went along (from a middle rail), as opposed to running on limited battery power.

1882: The year that streamlining became an option in the design of trains. Samuel W. Johnson's Midland Railway 'Spinners' looked sleek and elegant in their maroon casings, and for the first time hid a locomotive's mechanical workings and underpinnings from passengers.

1882: The first running of the world-famous Orient Express, from Paris to Vienna.

1883: The world's first public-service electric railway was opened by British engineer Magnus Volk along Brighton seafront on England's south coast. It remains the oldest operating electric railway in the world. That same year, the Mödling and Hinterbrühl tram system in Austria became the first electric railway to be powered from overhead lines.

1890: The City and South London Railway opened the world's first deep-level electric railway and passengers breathed a smoke-free sigh of relief.

1890: The Forth Rail Bridge opened. At 1.5 miles long, it was the biggest bridge in the world and created a short cut for trains from London and Edinburgh to Aberdeen. The amount of maintenance required (then and now) has coined the colloquial expression 'painting the Forth Bridge' as a way of describing a never-ending task.

NAVVIES

In the first 50 years of railway building in Britain alone, millions of navvies dug through enough earth and rock to create a network that was the equivalent of digging to Australia and back. Multiply that effort to create the railways of the world, and it is no surprise that they earned a reputation as hard, tough men. In fact, they started off as navigators (hence 'navvies'), as they were often the only people who could figure out the way across difficult terrain. So they weren't exactly daft either.

THE MEANING OF TIME

Around the turn of the twentieth century Belfast Railway Station, in deference to the political sensitivities prevailing at the time, displayed two different times on the same clock dial: Dublin Mean Time (which was 25 minutes 21 seconds behind GMT) and Belfast Mean Time (which was 23 minutes 39 seconds behind GMT). It follows that passengers had to adjust their watches by 1 minute 42 seconds whenever they crossed the border between north and south, even though there wasn't any border at the time!

THE UPS AND DOWNS OF THE TWENTIETH CENTURY

By 1900 there were 22,000 miles of railway track in Britain alone, and the next 20 years are now considered by many to be the golden age of the train, with thousands of iconic railway posters extolling the virtues of destinations around the world, from Italy's

Amalfi Coast to the Canadian Rockies, from England's Lake District to India's Taj Mahal. Almost all journeys between cities in the developed world took place by train at speeds of up to 90 mph. Motor cars and aeroplanes were not yet ready to provide competition. Those who could afford it travelled in trains that had sleeping and dining cars, lavatories, electric light and even an onboard barber service. By now, even third-class carriages must have seemed impossibly grand to the working classes, the polished wood and glazed windows a far cry from the open-top cattle-trucks they had originally been given to stop them getting ideas above their station.

But the century as a whole would not run smoothly for the railways, with two world wars to contend with and the need to modernise in the face of fierce competition from developing road and air transport systems.

1904: The original route of the Trans-Siberian Railway from Moscow to Vladivostok was completed.

1908: The Great Northern Railway produced its famous Jolly Fisherman advertising poster with the 'Skegness Is So Bracing' slogan.

THE SWEET SORROW OF PARTING

A 1906 railway by-law in Britain prevented male persons above or 'apparently above' the age of eight years from travelling in any compartment reserved for the exclusive use of female passengers. This must have been a difficult period for older-looking 8-year-olds, many of whom never saw their mothers again (not really).

1912: The world's first diesel-powered locomotive, using an engine designed by the eponymous German engineer and inventor Rudolf Diesel, was delivered to the Prussian State Railway in Berlin.

1914–18: Railways played a hugely important role in the transportation of troops and munitions throughout World War One.

WORLD WAR ONE TRAIN FACTS

➤ Widespread sabotage of their own railways by the Belgians greatly hindered Germany's initial invasion plan and gave France and Britain time to mobilise their own troops by train (including the French troops who were brought back from North Africa by the trainload).

➤ As all German troop trains had to go through Belgium to get to the front line in France, the British encouraged Belgian citizens to spy on them by posing as trainspotters. Many were caught and executed, but others found ingenious ways of getting the information back to the Allies, such as pole-vaulting over the electric barbed wire put up by the Germans.

➤ The roll-on/roll-off ferries that were used to transport trainloads of supplies across the English Channel to the Western Front during World War One played a vital part in securing victory. Shells manufactured in Britain in the morning could be fired direct from a railway gun in Belgium or France that afternoon without ever leaving the track.

➤ Railways were vital on all sides to the supply of everything from troops and munitions to tanks and trucks, food and beer rations, medical staff and bandages, horses and their fodder, and the all-important letters and food parcels from home.

➤ Trains were used to get soldiers home on leave, repatriate the dead, evacuate the wounded and send prisoners home at the end of the war.

➤ Because keeping tracks, bridges and tunnels open was strategically vital, military railway companies were set up to provide infrastructure all the way to the front lines.

➤ In Britain alone, 60,000 women carried out the railway jobs left behind by the men who had gone off to fight.

➤ A railway carriage played host to the end of the conflict, when the Armistice of 11 November 1918 was signed in French Commander Ferdinand Foch's former Orient Express railway carriage headquarters at Compiègne in the Ardennes forest north of Paris.

➤ Germany had to hand over around 7,500 locomotives and 2,000 freight trains as part of the peace terms.

'THE INVASION ON PLATFORM ONE IS RUNNING AHEAD OF SCHEDULE'

Germany's initial plan in 1914 was to invade France by train through neutral Luxembourg and Belgium. On 1 August 1914 it was decided that the invasion of Luxembourg would be delayed until the following day, but an advance guard of 16 German troops didn't get the telegram until it was too late. They turned up at Troisvierges railway station in Luxembourg, where the locals got to know that World War One was about to start the night before anyone else did. One hour later the German troops were recalled when the telegram finally arrived, resulting in one of the shortest invasions in history. They invaded again the next morning, this time on schedule, and Luxembourg's railways were soon under the Kaiser's control.

1917: The Trans-Australian Railway was completed, linking Western Australia with the rest of the country to the east, and therefore all the way to Sydney.

1920s: Germany led the way as the world's train builders got to grips with diesel-powered technology. Diesel fuelled the transmission system, which in turn powered the wheels, i.e. similar to motor-car technology. These impressive new locomotives could be started with the turn of a key and did not require the carrying of vast quantities of coal and water.

THE BOGIE MEN

Crucial to the development of diesel and, later, electric locomotives was the need for designers to come up with simpler wheel arrangements than those used on steam locomotives. They came up with bogies that allowed the fixed frame of the locomotive or carriage above to 'swivel' when the train was cornering. The main bogie arrangements designed to carry diesel and electric locomotives are known as Bo-Bo (two four-wheeled bogies, one at either end) and Co-Co (two six-wheeled bogies, one at either end).

1922: Inauguration of the service that became famously known as *The Blue Train* (*Le Train Bleu*) from Calais to the Côte d'Azur. This was a reincarnation of the *Calais Méditerranée Express* that had run to the French Riviera from 1886 until the outbreak of war in 1914.

1932: The diesel-powered *Fliegender Hamburger* (*Flying Hamburger*) came into service between Hamburg and Berlin, the fastest regular service in the world at the time, with a top speed of 99 mph.

1934: The *Burlington (Pioneer) Zephyr* entered service on the Chicago, Burlington and Quincy Railroad in the American Midwest. It was the first of the iconic stainless-steel diesel streamliners that captured the American public's imagination for the next 40 years.

1937: In the USA, General Motors started to mass-produce streamlined diesel-electric locomotives for the Union Pacific Railroad. Managing to look simultaneously powerful and Disney-esque (on account of their cartoon-dog faces, which the Americans referred to as 'bulldog-nosed'), they changed the face and sound of rail travel and heralded the ultimate demise of steam.

1938: In Britain the London and North Eastern Railway A4 Class *Mallard*, designed by Nigel Gresley, set a world speed record for steam trains of 126 mph. The record still stands.

1939–45: Trains were again vital to the movement of troops and munitions on all sides, and women on both sides of the Atlantic again took on the railway jobs of the men who went off to fight.

WORLD WAR TWO TRAIN FACTS

➤ The inhabitants of major cities in Europe took shelter in their underground train stations during bombing raids.

➤ In 1940, Hitler rubbed salt into French wounds at Compiègne by forcing them to surrender in the same former Orient Express carriage in which Germany had been made to sign the Armistice in 1918. The carriage had to be brought from a Paris museum for the purpose.

➤ Over 3 million people, mostly children, were evacuated by train from the British cities that were bombing targets for the Luftwaffe during the Battle of Britain in 1940.

➤ The biggest traveller numbers in US history transpired in the three years following the bombing of Pearl Harbor in December 1941, as troops were carried across the continent to the ports that would transport them to the European and Pacific theatres of war.

➤ The Burma Railway, also known as the Death Railway, was completed under Japanese command in 1943 to supply their Burma campaign from Thailand. They used Asian labour and Allied prisoners of war, who were forced to work under appalling conditions not only to build the railway but also to rebuild Bridge 277 (the bridge over the River Kwai) every time the Allies bombed it.

➤ Nazi Germany made the most dreadful use of trains imaginable to transport millions to their death, but trains also saved lives, including the 10,000 Jewish children evacuated to Britain on the Kindertransport (children transport) trains before the outbreak of war. They were met by foster parents at Liverpool Street Station in London, outside which a memorial was erected in 2006 to commemorate the rescue mission.

1941: The world's biggest-ever locomotives, the appropriately named *Big Boys*, were built to go into stream-driven service to haul freight on the Union Pacific Railroad in the USA; although diesel-electric technology had by now arrived to stay, the proven technology of steam locomotion would continue to exist alongside it for a while yet.

1948: Britain's railway system was nationalised.

1955: British Rail announced its Modernisation Plan, sounding the death knell for steam and heralding a bright new future of US-style diesel and (eventually) French-style electric trains. A deterioration in service followed, because the initial diesel trains proved less reliable and slower than the steam trains they replaced.

1957: For the first time in the USA, more passengers travelled by plane than by train.

MADE TO LAST

Between 1825 and 1960 around 130,000 steam locomotives were built in Britain at 22 different factories, from Brighton to Inverness. Most were built in Glasgow (25,600), followed by Manchester (20,500) and Leeds (12,100), and many were exported around the globe.

The last one to be built (at Swindon Works in Wiltshire) was 92220 *Evening Star*, a 2-10-0 Standard Class 9F, the only locomotive to be earmarked for preservation before production even started. Having served its time in the 1960s, it continues to enjoy pride of place at the National Railway Museum in York, playing out the role it was always destined to fulfil: that of an important museum exhibit.

1963: In Britain, the infamous Beeching Report was published, in which Dr Richard Beeching, the then chairman of British Rail, announced the decommissioning of many rural branch lines.

THE B WORD

Although the railway network in Britain had been built in a fairly random fashion in an age when cars didn't exist, and was probably therefore in need of a certain amount of rationalisation, the name Beeching nonetheless became synonymous with short-sighted politics. This was partly because the cost savings heralded in his 1963 report to Parliament never materialised, and partly because the twentieth-century obsession to switch traffic from rail to road would prove somewhat wrongheaded, but mostly because the rural communities affected would feel deeply resentful for many years at being abandoned by the system.

1964: The first high-speed electric Shinkansen service, the so-called bullet train, started up in Japan, running between Tokyo and Osaka.

1965: Following the state funeral of Winston Churchill, his body was, appropriately, transported behind the Battle of Britain class locomotive *Winston Churchill* from London Waterloo to Hanborough, Oxfordshire, the nearest station to his burial place in the village of Bladon.

1967: The high-speed electric service run by Société Nationale des Chemins de Fer Français (SNCF) between Paris and Toulouse, known as *Le Capitole*, became the first train in Europe to be scheduled to run at 200 km/h (124 mph).

1968: British Rail ran the last steam train on its network and banned all railway preservation societies from doing the same, so anyone with a steam engine had to take it to a preserved branch line.

1971: The US Congress created the nationalised Amtrak passenger network and eliminated numerous unprofitable routes.

1976: British Rail introduced the InterCity 125 high-speed diesel, so-called because its top operational cruising speed was 125 mph. Its absolute maximum speed of 148 mph has remained a world record for a diesel-powered train since its inception.

1981: The first electric TGV (*Train à Grande Vitesse*) ran from Paris to Lyon, setting the 200-mph standard for conventional high-speed trains that has applied ever since.

1987: Opening of the fully automated (driverless) Docklands Light Railway in London.

1988: The ETR (ElettroTrenoRapido) 450, also known as the 'Pendolino' (meaning 'little pendulum'), became the first 'active tilting' train in the world to enter into regular service, between Milan and Rome.

TO TILT OR NOT TO TILT, THAT IS THE QUESTION

As the Japanese and the French built dedicated high-speed networks alongside their existing tracks in the 1970s and 1980s, the rest of the world looked on with envy. Those who couldn't afford new dedicated lines, or whose terrain didn't suit, had to come up with an alternative, and tilting trains provided it, because they are able to take corners on existing lines much faster than the slower trains the lines were designed for in the first place. Tilting trains are now widely used throughout Europe and Asia. In Britain, tilting trains are used to speed round the many tight curves of the West Coast Line from London to Glasgow, but are not so necessary on the much flatter and straighter East Coast Line from London to Edinburgh.

1994: The Channel Tunnel opened, connecting continental Europe to the United Kingdom for the first time. Following subsequent upgrades to the UK end of the line, Eurostar now runs a service from London to Paris in 2 hours 15 minutes and from London to Brussels in 1 hour 51 minutes, while Eurotunnel operates Le Shuttle service for cars and lorries (and their passengers) from Folkestone to Calais in 35 minutes.

1996: The French TGVs were so successful at getting short-haul airline passengers back onto the rails that SNCF needed to introduce double-decker trains (the TGV Duplex) to cope with demand.

1997: Britain's passenger and freight railways were privatised and broken up into a number of smaller operating companies. A separate infrastructure provider (currently Network Rail) was given responsibility for the provision and maintenance of the 20,000 miles of track, 40,000 bridges and tunnels, and 2,500 railway stations.

RAIL TRAVEL IN THE TWENTY-FIRST CENTURY

High-speed 'floating' trains grab the headlines in the twenty-first century, and environmental awareness plays an increasingly significant role in the maintenance and expansion of railway networks. Electrification continues to proliferate for those who can afford the infrastructure, and biodiesel is of increasing interest to those who can't.

But high speed is only appropriate for long-distance travel, not for urban rail systems, without which the major cities of the world would simply grind to a halt. Over 160 cities around the world now rely on urban systems that operate above or below ground with or without human drivers.

2003: Australia's second transcontinental railway finally linked Darwin in the north with Adelaide in the south.

2004: The first commercial high-speed maglev (magnetic levitation) service began in China, with a line that links Shanghai International Airport to the Shanghai Metro.

2006: The amount of the world's rail traffic being carried over electrified networks reached 50 per cent.

2007: A redeveloped St Pancras Station was opened in London to provide the new Eurostar terminus for trains to and from Paris and Brussels.

2007: In Britain, the Royal Train completed a 900-mile return journey from London to Scarborough on biodiesel alone.

HIS ROYAL GREENNESS

Many rail companies continue to experiment with running trains on a mixture of biodiesel and regular diesel, but that was never going to be enough for His Royal Highness, the Prince of Wales. Already well known for his sustainable farming methods in Britain, his 2007 experiment to run the Royal Train on a combination of waste rapeseed and sunflower oil alone proved that Prince Charles is also a trailblazer in the field of green fuel.

In 2009 Disneyland California followed the royal lead with the announcement that it would run all its trains on its own waste vegetable cooking oil, and in recent years the Mount Washington Cog Railway in New Hampshire has been converting its steam locomotives to run on biodiesel. The future is looking green, and very oily.

2008: The first new steam locomotive to be built since 1960 was completed at Darlington Locomotive Works in England. It is a Peppercorn Class A1 4-6-2 Pacific steam locomotive, which is used to run special services on the mainline railways of Britain. (Peppercorn locomotives were originally built in 1948–49 and were so named after their designer, Arthur Peppercorn, the last Chief Mechanical Engineer of the London and North Eastern Railway.)

2009: Work began on the multibillion London Crossrail project to deliver 62 miles of east–west track from Reading and Heathrow Airport in the west to Abbey Wood in the east, including 26 miles of tunnels under the capital itself.

COME ON, GIRLS, YOU CAN DO IT!

Eight 150-metre-long tunnel-boring machines, working in pairs, are being used on the London Crossrail project to excavate 4 million tonnes of material that will then be recycled to create a new RSPB (Royal Society for the Protection of Birds) nature reserve at Wallasea Island in Essex. Following tradition, the tunnelling machines are named after important female figures, on this occasion with strong connections to London:

Victoria and Elizabeth: Queens at the time of the first great railway age and the Crossrail project respectively.

Ada and Phyllis: Ada Lovelace, an early computer scientist who wrote the first computer program, and Phyllis Pearsall, who single-handedly created the London A–Z.

Mary and Sophia: wives of Isambard Kingdom Brunel, who built the Great Western Railway, and Marc Isambard Brunel, who built the first tunnel under the River Thames.

———————

Jessica and Ellie: Jessica Ennis-Hill, gold-medal heptathlete at the London 2012 Olympics, and Ellie Simmonds, multiple-gold-medal swimmer at the Paralympic Games of Beijing 2008 and London 2012.

EVERY TRAIN UNDER THE SUN

In 2014 the redeveloped Blackfriars Station in London became the first to have platforms extending out over the River Thames, under cover of the world's largest bridge to be covered entirely with solar panels, which will provide 50 per cent of the station's energy requirements.

2013: China achieved over 6,000 miles of high-speed network, the largest such network in the world.

QUELLE SURPRISE!

The idea of a Channel Tunnel between England and France took forever to get off the ground (or, should I say, to get underground), partly on account of earlier nineteenth-century attempts failing on technical grounds, partly because of public opposition and political apathy on the part of the British for most of the twentieth century. It has, therefore, come as something of a surprise to learn that over 80 per cent of passengers using the Eurostar and Le Shuttle services today are British, the people who didn't really want it.

2014: Channel Tunnel operator Eurostar unveiled the e320 high-speed train, so called because it can travel at up to 320 km/h (200 mph), and the introduction of direct routes to Marseille (from 2015) and Amsterdam (from 2016).

RIDING THE RAILWAYS OF THE WORLD

We would like to apologise to passengers for the delay of the incoming train from Nagoya. This train will now arrive eleven seconds late.

Heard on a platform at
Kyoto Station in Japan

One of the great things about the railways of the world is that they are all so very different. Developed independently to meet the needs of their own country's geography, population and culture, they were also subject, of course, to what their governments or industries could afford.

Railway designers and engineers have found various ingenious solutions to the challenges of different terrains, such that railways can travel overground, underground and even above ground. Indeed, some track gauges are more suited to one terrain than another, with narrow gauge being ideally suited to climbing mountains, for example, but not much use for hauling mile-long freight trains across an entire continent. It follows that the size of trains used by railway companies is determined by the configuration of their networks, i.e. not just the width between its rails (track gauge) but also the dimensions of its platforms, tunnels and bridges (loading gauge).

Electrified networks are prevalent on railways that can afford the infrastructure and have the right terrain for it, and diesel remains the power source of choice for most of the others. Steam, though, has not gone away, primarily because a determined number of people remain committed to preserving what many still refer to as the golden age of the railway.

In this chapter we will look at the current state of some of the many different railways of the world, starting where it all began, in Britain.

> *The train now arriving on platform*
> *one is on fire. Passengers are*
> *advised not to board this train.*

Announced at Bournemouth Station in Dorset

THE RAILWAYS OF BRITAIN

 Today there are 23 passenger networks run by a dozen or so operating companies in Britain, from the old railway giants like First Great Western – the Great Western Railway as was – to the much newer kids on the block like Virgin Trains. Some networks are regional affairs, e.g. Southeastern, ScotRail, Arriva Trains Wales, whereas others stretch the length and/or breadth of the country, e.g. East Coast Main Line, CrossCountry Trains (who have the longest network of all, as well as the longest direct line, which runs from Aberdeen in Scotland to Penzance in Cornwall). Some are much more specific in their range and purpose, e.g. British Airport Authority's Heathrow Express, or Eurostar's line out to France and Belgium.

Huge freightliner trains carrying goods to and from container docks like those at Felixstowe remain an essential part of industry, increasingly so as British roads become ever more clogged up by cars and lorries alike. The largest rail freight company is now the massive German firm DB Schenker, after it bought out EWS (English, Welsh and Scottish Railways) in 2007.

The coming years will see huge investment in high-speed trains and electrification of lines, and tilting trains will continue to be needed to negotiate the many twists and turns up and down the west of the country. Diesel will continue to power trains where electrification is not possible or sensible, with increasing use of biodiesel a real possibility to further protect the environment. The Crossrail project and the rebuilding of London Bridge Station are due to ease congestion across London by 2018. In the meantime, commuters into and out of the city will continue to suffer on overcrowded trains that often struggle to run on time on a network that was, after all, built for the Victorian age.

Facts and figures:

➤ The fastest trains on the British rail network are those used on the Eurostar service to France and Belgium, followed by the appropriately named British Rail Class 395 'Javelin', introduced to cope with the increased demand for high-speed services at the time of the London 2012 Olympics.

➤ Around 40 per cent of British track is electrified, due to rise to 50 per cent by 2020.

➤ Seventy per cent of all journeys begin or end in one of London's 13 mainline terminals.

➤ London Waterloo has the most platforms of any British station (20) and is the country's busiest station in terms of passenger numbers (over 90 million per annum).

➤ Clapham Junction, in London, is Europe's busiest rail station in terms of traffic, with trains running through it every 13 seconds during peak hours and every 30 seconds at off-peak times.

➤ Colchester Station in Essex has the longest platform in Britain, at 620 metres.

➤ There are over 150 heritage railways in Britain, an appropriately high number for the home of rail.

➤ Llanfairpwllgwyngyllgogerychwyrndrobw-
lllllantysiliogogogoch on the Isle of Anglesey
in North Wales is, not surprisingly, the railway
station with the longest name in Britain. Its
English translation is 'St Mary's church in
the hollow of the white hazel near a rapid
whirlpool and the church of St Tysilio of the
red cave'.

➤ There are around 150 request stops at small
stations around the British mainland. If you
don't put your hand out, the train doesn't
stop.

RONALD McDONALD ON THE LINE

Trains were delayed in south Wales when
an 8-metre inflatable Ronald McDonald
was reported to be blocking the line ahead.
Ronald had flown off the roof of the nearby
McDonalds restaurant in Newport after
staff had apparently overcompensated for
his previous deflated condition.

WINDSOR AND (NOT) ETON

There is a station in Berkshire called Windsor and Eton Central, but it most certainly is not. Eton does not have its own railway station because the famous school felt threatened by the arrival of the railways in the nineteenth century and lobbied parliament to build the 'Eton kink', a giant curve in the track that takes a wide berth around the school to this day. The school's concerns were that their untrustworthy pupils (mostly future prime ministers of Britain plus a few of the world's other despots) were bound to throw stones at passing trains and pick fights with the train-travelling lower classes.

THE RAILWAYS OF FRANCE

 The French have been rather good at running railways. From the outset, in 1842, the government decided on a national strategy, thereby largely avoiding the piecemeal and poorly structured networks of many other countries, including Britain. The infrastructure consisted of several major lines radiating out from Paris, plus a cross-country line along the south of the country and a north–south line along the western edge of the Alps. The network was designed to serve as many towns and cities as possible and continues to serve them well to this day. When the time came to rein in the network in the face of competition from road and air in the twentieth century, the French pruned in sensible fashion, even keeping metre-gauge lines running where there was good reason to do so, such as in the Alps and the Pyrenees and also in Corsica.

Their sensible infrastructure again stood them in good stead when they took the decision to move towards high-speed electrification in the 1970s. As they laid down purpose-built track alongside the existing network lines, many railways around the world looked on in envy as one TGV after another took to the fast, straight lines. When the time came in 1994 to link up with Britain via *Le Tunnel sous la Manche*, their trains inevitably ran faster on their own tracks than they could on the slower British tracks on the other side.

Facts and figures:

➤ The Gare du Nord in Paris is Europe's busiest station in terms of passenger numbers (up to 180 million per annum).

➤ The national railway company (SNCF) runs more than 800 TGV services a day over approximately 1,200 miles of high-speed track.

➤ TGV technology has now been adopted in several European countries and as far afield as South Korea and Taiwan.

THE RAILWAYS OF GERMANY

With inventors like Werner von Siemens and Rudolf Diesel at its disposal, it is hardly surprising that Germany led the way with the early development of electrified railways and, later, with diesel locomotives. Nowadays, its growing fleet of ICE (InterCity Express) trains (designed and built, of course, by Siemens) speed across its growing high-speed electric network and beyond into neighbouring European countries.

The current incarnation of Deutsche Bahn came into existence in 1994 as the unified successor to the former state railways of West and East Germany. The largest rail company in Europe, it carries around

2 billion passengers a year. It also includes DB Schenker, the largest freight operator in Europe, whose operating network spans territory from Portugal to Russia and from Sweden to Turkey.

Facts and figures:

➤ Munich Hauptbahnhof (Central Station) has the most platforms of any station in Europe, with 34 plus another six to serve the U-Bahn.

➤ An average of 12,874 glasses of beer are served on Deutsche Bahn trains every day.

➤ Deutsche Bahn is headquartered in Berlin and is the jersey sponsor of local football team Hertha Berlin, its DB logo proudly displayed on the players' chests.

➤ On 10 November 1989, the day after the Berlin Wall fell, thousands of East Berliners, scarcely able to believe their luck, lined up at Berlin Friedrichstrasse Bahnhof to take the short train journey into West Berlin.

A PROPER TRAIN ROBBER

Jesse James and Butch Cassidy found fame and fortune as the most successful train robbers of America's Wild West, but neither of them took to stealing whole trains. That was left to an unidentified train robber in Berlin in 2010. Whoever he was, he turned up at the Deutches Technikmuseum (German Museum of Technology) claiming to be the owner of two locomotives and a carriage that had been on loan to the museum for a while. Museum staff promptly handed over the keys and the trains were never seen again. Perhaps the culprit didn't leave any tracks the police could follow?

ITALIAN DESIGN

Italy was an early adopter of electrification, having no coal deposits to draw on (for that same reason, it had been particularly happy when Alessandro Volta invented the battery). It continues to make very good use of that mode of power on its high-speed networks today.

Sleek Italian design has also been ideal for streamlining trains. Starting with the groundbreaking Bugatti Autorails of the 1930s, impressive designs have continued with the likes of Fiat's Pendolino tilting trains (now used around the world) and state-owned Trenitalia's bang-up-to-date *Frecciarossa* (*Red Arrow*), the main competitor of which is the privately owned, Ferrari-inspired Italo. Pininfarina is another Italian company that has branched out from car and bicycle design to that of trains, including the interior refurbishment and exterior livery design of a new Eurostar fleet.

> ## 'SAY WHAT YOU LIKE ABOUT MUSSOLINI, AT LEAST HE GOT ALL THE TRAINS TO RUN ON TIME.'
>
> He didn't really. It was largely a propaganda myth and, in fact, there were lots of accounts of late-running trains during his time in power. What he was good at was turning up to take the credit every time a new station, tunnel or bridge opened up on the Italian railway system, but he was no better at running railways than he was at choosing winning sides.

THE RAILWAYS OF SWITZERLAND

 The Swiss got railways right from the start and a combination of stable government and neutrality in war has left its solid infrastructure intact ever since. With no indigenous fuel supply and much of its terrain in any event unsuited to steam or diesel, electricity was the clear and only solution from the outset.

They built their own locomotives to a simple design that has stood the test of time, but the engineering required to cross gorges and cut through mountains was anything but simple. As pioneers of reinforced concrete, they dug and arched their way through the Alps, with the added joy that their infrastructure was (and is) as elegant as it was functional. Tunnels aside, it goes without saying that the scenery to be viewed from Alpine train journeys is hard to beat.

Facts and figures:

➤ The recently built Gotthard Base Tunnel under the Swiss Alps is the world's longest mainline railway tunnel.

➤ The Swiss railways' reputation for punctuality arises from their ability to run their trains like clockwork – like their own precise clockwork, in fact.

➤ The Jungfraubahn railway in the Berner Oberland region runs to the highest railway station in Europe.

GETTING TO THE CORE OF THE MATTER

The numberless Swiss railway clock, with its red second hand in the shape of a railway guard's signalling disc (used to tell the train driver he can leave), was designed in 1944 by Swiss engineer Hans Hilfiker and soon became a (patented) national icon. The Apple company inadvertently used the design on its iOS 6 operating system in 2012 and reportedly had to pay over $20 million to the Swiss Federal Railway to regularise its licensing position.

THE RAILWAYS OF RUSSIA

Not surprisingly for such a vast country, Russia has one of the largest rail networks in the world, even after allowing for the fact that two-fifths of it was lost when the USSR broke up in 1991. Its mainline runs on 1.5-metre broad gauge, but it also has a lot of narrow-gauge track to serve its port areas and some of its less hospitable terrain.

Russia is hardly at the forefront of high-speed railway development, but it has made a decent start with its *Sapsan* (*Peregrine Falcon*) fast trains on the Moscow–St Petersburg and Moscow–Nizhny Novgorod (Gorky, as was) lines, and with the *Allegro* on the cross-border St Petersburg–Helsinki line.

Facts and figures:

➤ All Russian trains run to Moscow time, to avoid the confusion that would otherwise arise from timetables having to span up to five time zones.

➤ Russian gauge (still in use throughout the ex-USSR and in Finland) is the second most common gauge in the world, after standard gauge. It is believed that this broad gauge was initially chosen in 1842 for fear of rail invasions by standard-gauge neighbours.

➤ State-of-the-art double-decker trains with on-board Wi-Fi were introduced on the Moscow–Sochi line in time for the 2014 Winter Olympics.

➤ In March 1917 Nicholas II, the last tsar of Russia, was forced to abdicate on board the royal train at Pskov Station near the present-day border with Estonia.

➤ Shortly after the Tsar's abdication in 1917, Vladimir Lenin entered St Petersburg in triumph in the famous 'Sealed Train' that secured his safe passage through war-torn Europe. The train was provided by the Germans, along with gold worth \$10 million, in the hope that Lenin could put an end to Russian opposition to Germany on the Eastern Front.

THE BROAD-MINDED, NARROW-MINDED SPANISH

Spain took an early decision to adopt a broad gauge, a disastrous mistake for a poor country that could not at the time afford to maintain or expand its network. It also rendered itself incompatible with the rest of Europe, other than its neighbour Portugal (which shared the so-called Iberian gauge). Away from the main lines, it filled the rest of the country with narrow-gauge track more suited to the majority of its terrain, thereby rendering the main lines incompatible with the rural network.

In the twenty-first century there is only good news, though, as Spain has done more than just catch up with its European neighbours; it has, in fact, created the largest high-speed (standard-gauge!) network on the Continent, allowing it to cater for international traffic and to meet the demands of its own growing fleet of impressive AVE (*Alta Velocidad Española*) trains.

THE RAILROADS OF THE USA

Ever since the Baltimore and Ohio Railroad carried its first passengers in 1830, the railroads have played a huge part in American history. They helped to tame the Wild West and to physically connect the peoples of this vast landmass, at the same time helping Americans to build a sense of their national identity. Today, government-owned Amtrak is the national passenger rail network, with 30 train routes linking 500 destinations across 46 states, but a whopping 80 per cent of the country's network is given over to freight, most of which is transported by the privately owned Union Pacific and BNSF (Burlington Northern Santa Fe) railroad companies.

Diesel has long been king on the railroads of America, with one impressively muscular locomotive after another hauling its freight or passengers over huge distances. Unsurprisingly, many of these giants found their way into the films of Hollywood, alongside the earlier steam trains of the USA and Europe. In recognition of the need for speed, efficiency and environmental care in the twenty-first century, however, a national high-speed electric network of around 17,000 miles is planned to be in place by 2030, the first phase of which will be completed in California.

Facts and figures:

➤ The USA has by far the largest rail network in the world, with 155,350 miles of track.

➤ The Union Pacific and BNSF are amongst the largest freight railroads in the world. The Union Pacific alone has 8,300 locomotives hauling freight across 23 states.

➤ Wyoming and South Dakota are the only two of the 48 contiguous states not served by Amtrak (apparently not enough people want to go there by train to justify the business case).

➤ Penn Station in New York City handles more passengers than any other station in the USA, with up to a thousand passengers every 90 seconds.

EAST IS EAST AND WEST IS WEST

The romantic notion of linking the USA and Russia with a rail bridge or tunnel across the 58-mile Bering Strait between Alaska and Siberia has been talked about for over a hundred years. In 2011, the *Daily Mail* in Britain reported that the Russian government had agreed to put up $60 billion of the estimated $100 billion required, but there is no sign of the Americans putting up the rest or having the political will to join landmasses with their old Cold War foes.

THE RAILWAYS OF JAPAN

 Somewhat ironically given its modern-day propensity for speed, the Japanese railway system was built on a relatively slow narrow gauge of 1 metre because of its mountainous terrain – although, in 1959, one of its trains did set a narrow-gauge world speed record of 101 mph. It remains largely narrow gauge to this day, except, of course, for its high-speed lines, which required standard gauge from the outset. Since the first Shinkansen (bullet train) ran in 1964, the high-speed network has expanded to around 1,500 miles.

There is a cultural obsession in Japan with trains running on time, including announcements of trains being so many seconds late and, worse still, hour-long delays making newspaper headlines. This national neurosis is even thought to be responsible for accidents caused by drivers determined to make up delays of as little as a minute. It seems certain that this ongoing preoccupation with speed and punctuality will drive the country into the 'maglev age' with no small amount of enthusiasm. Japan already holds the world speed record, set in 2003 when one of its prototype maglev trains achieved 361 mph.

Facts and figures:

➤ The Shinjuku Station complex in Tokyo handles more passengers than any other station in the world, having over 200 entrances/exits to control a flow of up to 4 million passengers a day.

➤ The longest undersea railway tunnel in the world is the Seikan Tunnel linking the two main islands of Japan, Honshu and Hokkaido. It runs for 33.46 miles under the Tsugaru Strait.

➤ In 1921 the Japanese prime minister, Hara Takashi, was stabbed to death in Tokyo Station by a railway employee who did not share his political views.

➤ The *ekiben* is a pre-packed bento lunchbox that has been sold on Japanese railway stations and trains for over a hundred years. Its place in Japanese culture may be under threat as more and more high-speed train journeys don't last long enough for passengers to require lunch on board.

THE RAILWAYS OF CHINA

 Chinese railways had a rather inauspicious start in the nineteenth century when the intransigent ruling mandarins, who felt threatened by encroaching modernity, decided to show the public how dangerous trains could be by throwing bound labourers in front of them. The mandarins responded to the inevitable public outcry by buying up the railways and destroying them.

Long periods of war and revolution ensured that subsequent railway systems continued to stagnate until the latter half of the twentieth century. In 1950, a country with double the landmass of America and five times its population had only 3 per cent as much track. Ensuing Communist regimes then decided that enough was enough, and recent decades have seen a remarkable turnaround, as the Chinese leadership has harnessed all the engineering prowess it could muster, along with an inexhaustible supply of cheap labour, to achieve unparalleled network growth and unrivalled feats of railway engineering across very difficult terrain.

That momentum has continued into the twenty-first century. China now has the second-largest network in the world (after the USA), and the largest high-speed network on the planet. It is also at the forefront of the futuristic maglev technology, having inaugurated the world's first commercial service in 2004 to connect Shanghai Airport with the Shanghai Metro system at Pudong.

Facts and figures:

➤ Rail is the principal method of transport in China.

➤ The world's longest high-speed railway line runs for 1,428 miles between Beijing and Guangzhou.

➤ The longest bridge in the world is the Danyang–Kunshan Grand Bridge, built to accommodate the Beijing–Shanghai high-speed railway (as was the second longest bridge in the world, at Tianjin).

➤ The highest stretch of railway in the world is at Tanggula Pass, 5,072 metres above sea level, being the highest point of the track that runs from Xining in Qinghai Province to Lhasa in Tibet. Personal oxygen supplies are given to passengers to prevent altitude sickness.

➤ Chinese railways follow the pattern of British-style raised platforms and the driving of trains on the left-hand side of dual track (as opposed to the American style of track-level boarding and right-hand drive).

THE RAILWAYS OF INDIA

Although rail travel was introduced to India in the mid nineteenth century so that the British could move more freely around the jewel in their imperial crown, Indian Railways had become a very Indian affair long before independence in 1947, thanks to a longstanding policy of local recruitment and management handover.

The company has long been one of the world's largest employers (with over 1.5 million employees), carrying more than 23 million passengers a day across 39,000 miles of track to 6,800 different stations. Travelling conditions range from first-class, air-conditioned luxury to suburban commuting where personal space is not offered at any price, a problem that has been exacerbated by the relatively recent outlawing of hanging off the side or sitting cross-legged on top of trains. On many lines, live overhead cables had rather taken the fun out of sitting up top in any event.

The British not only bequeathed a legacy of robust, long-distance, broad-gauge railways; they also left behind a number of very different narrow-gauge mountain railways, built in whatever way was necessary to get them up to their respective hill stations to escape the fierce heat of the Indian summer. These included Simla (the hot-weather retreat from Delhi), Darjeeling (to escape Calcutta, now Kolkata), Matheran (to escape Bombay, now Mumbai) and Ooty (to escape Madras, now Chennai).

Facts and figures:

➤ There are no high-speed trains in India.

➤ Indian railways run predominantly on a broad gauge of 1.435 metres, which is more suited to the heavy trains required to haul high volumes of passengers and freight.

➤ Double-decker trains are being introduced around the country in a further attempt to cope with the high demand for passenger services.

➤ The longest route in India is the *Vivek Express*, which runs from the north-eastern state of Assam to the very southern tip of the country in Tamil Nadu. It takes 82 hours 30 minutes to cover the 2,663 miles, which is an average speed of 32 mph. Not many countries would call that an express.

➤ The *Lifeline Express* is a hospital-on-wheels that provides healthcare to rural India, with one of the carriages set up as an operating room.

➤ Every day, 4,000 dabbawalas board trains to deliver 160,000 tiffin lunches, prepared at home by suburban wives and mothers, to the office workers of Mumbai.

➤ The longest railway platform in the world, at 1,366 metres, is at Gorakhpur Station in Uttar Pradesh.

➤ Meals served on Indian trains are described as either 'vegetarian' or 'non-vegetarian'. Indians have the lowest rate of meat consumption in the world, and the train companies have to balance their offerings accordingly.

THE RAILWAYS OF CENTRAL AND SOUTH AMERICA

 Neither Central nor South America have anything like an integrated railway network, but they do nonetheless have some outstanding lines dotted around the continent. Four of the highest six railways in the world, for example, are situated within South America: Peru has the *Tren de Sierra* from Lima to Huancayo and the *Andean Explorer* from Cuzco to Puno on Lake Titicaca; Bolivia has the Rio Mulatos–Potosí line; and the *Tren a las Nubes* (*Cloud Train*) runs across the Andes and the Atacama Desert to connect Salta in Argentina with Antofagasta on the coast of Chile. Peru, of course, also has the 54-mile rail journey to the destination on everybody's bucket list: Machu Picchu.

Facts and figures:

➤ The line from Lima to Huancayo in Peru had the highest stretch of railway in the world until this distinction was usurped by the Qinghai–Tibet Railway in 2006.

➤ The Southern Fuegian Railway in Tierra del Fuego, Argentina, is the southernmost operating railway in the world. Steam and diesel engines transport passengers along the narrow-gauge track to 'End of the World Station' 5 miles west of Ushuaia.

➤ The oldest and shortest transcontinental railway in the world is the Panama Canal Railroad. Running alongside the more famous canal, it takes just an hour to travel the 48 miles from Colón on the Atlantic to Panama City on the Pacific.

THE RAILWAYS OF AFRICA

 Although the railways of Africa are likely to remain disjointed for many years to come, the continent does nonetheless offer some of the most spectacular railway journeys on planet earth. Most people have heard of the luxury *Blue Train* and the Rovos Rail *Pride of Africa* services that have crossed Southern Africa in style for decades, and these continue to excite today.

In more recent times the *Shongololo Express* service (*shongololo* is Zulu for 'millipede') has added new luxury routes across a number of Southern African countries, these lines taking in some combination or other of Mozambique, Zimbabwe, Zambia, Swaziland, Botswana, Namibia and South Africa (with one route also extending into Tanzania in East Africa). Their optional *Peace Train* service offers the same luxury travel, but with a twist that allows passengers to spend 40 per cent of their time on voluntary projects designed to alleviate poverty and improve health, education and farming opportunities.

At the other end of the financial scale, a multitude of local and regional services around Africa offer the chance to experience very different rail journeys, whether your preferred travelling habitat is desert or rainforest, mountain or savannah.

Facts and figures:

➤ Getting freight, and in particular oil and minerals, to African ports is of much greater importance to local and national economies than providing commuter or tourist routes.

By way of example, the Rift Valley Railway of Kenya and Uganda is made up of 95 per cent freight and 5 per cent passenger traffic.

➤ Cecil Rhodes, the British colonialist who made a fortune from diamond mining in the nineteenth century, wanted to spend much of that fortune on the building of a Cape to Cairo railway. The project was beset with geographical and political problems from the outset and, for much the same reasons, his dream remains unrealised to this day.

➤ In Tunisia, the *Lézard Rouge* (*Red Lizard*) train is a unique way to see dry gorges occasionally dotted with lush greenery from a carriage that was previously used by the Bey of Tunisia to get to his summer palace.

➤ The easiest way to get around Morocco's royal cities, and to cross the High Atlas mountains, is to take the train from Marrakech to Fes (or vice versa) and stop off at Rabat and Meknes en route.

➤ One of the best ways to see the Nile Valley (and its antiquities) is to travel along it by train. The line runs south from Alexandria to Cairo and then south to Luxor and Aswan.

TRAINING TO BE A LAWYER

While working as a young lawyer in South Africa, Mohandas (later Mahatma) Gandhi was thrown off a first-class train carriage for being the wrong colour. It was one of the events that led him to adopt the stance of non-violent civil disobedience that was to inspire civil rights movements around the world and lead India to independence from Britain.

SOME OF THE
GREAT TRAINS

*I could have developed a new train,
had I stayed in the railways. It would
have looked like the AK-47 though.*

Mikhail Kalashnikov

Some great trains are generic, like the French TGV, and some are specific, like the great named locomotives of the steam age. Great trains are also great for different reasons, whether it be raw power, high speed, sheer luxury or pure romance. Some have been enshrined in literature and the arts; some have even made it on to the big screen. Some trains became such celebrities during their working lives that people travelled far and wide to see them.

I haven't been constrained by any particular definition of greatness in this chapter, but I have, however, been constrained by space, because great trains are many and we each have our personal favourites. I apologise in advance if yours does not get a mention.

LOCOMOTIVE NAMING AND NUMBERING

Different steam locomotives had different wheel arrangements, such that a 4-6-2 had four leading wheels, six driving wheels (coupled together) to power the train forward, and two trailing wheels. The driving wheels are very often huge in comparison to the other wheels.

In 1900 a Dutch-American engineer, Frederick Methven Whyte, decided to give names to these different wheel arrangements: a 4-6-2 became known as a Pacific, a 4-4-2 became an Atlantic, and so on. Although there are many exceptions to the general rules, you can be pretty sure that a 2-8-4 (Berkshire) locomotive wasn't used on the tight twists and turns of a narrow-gauge mountain railway, and you can be just as sure that a 0-6-0 (Six-coupled) locomotive (think Thomas the Tank Engine) was never used in an attempt to break the world speed record.

Individual railway companies, having chosen the wheel arrangement that best suited their needs, then set about building their own versions, or 'classes', of such locomotives (the wheels were just the wheels, they still needed to design the mechanics and the look and feel of their company's own trains). Each locomotive built within a class then had a number to distinguish it from the others built within that class, and many were given individual names as a final personal touch. By way of example, the first 4-6-2 Pacifics designed for the London and North Eastern Railway in the 1920s were designated A1 class, the most famous locomotive of which was numbered 4472 and named *Flying Scotsman*.

ROCKET

Designer:
Robert Stephenson
Built:
Newcastle upon Tyne, Tyne and Wear; 1829
Railway:
Liverpool and Manchester Railway
Power:
Steam
Wheel arrangement:
0-2-2 Northumbrian
Maximum speed:
28 mph
Main service life:
Liverpool to Manchester
Current whereabouts:
London Science Museum

This is the train that most historians consider the most important of all. When *Rocket* won the Rainhill locomotive trials as a prototype in 1829, it provided the template for the eight other locomotives due to be employed on the Liverpool to Manchester Railway from the following year onwards. *Rocket* itself operated on the line, having been upgraded from its prototype status, before switching in its dotage to Lord Carlisle's Railway, a branch line in Brampton, Cumberland (now Cumbria).

It was a distinctive-looking piece of engineering on account of its tall smokestack chimney and its single pair of large front driving wheels with two smaller trailing wheels behind. More importantly, the family of locomotives it spawned was impressively fast and reliable for the time.

The original *Rocket*, although much modified in the years following the Rainhill trials, can still be seen in all its finery at the Science Museum in London, while replicas exist at the National Railway Museum in York and, across the Atlantic, the Henry Ford Museum in Dearborn, Michigan and the Museum of Science and Industry in Chicago, Illinois. Buster Keaton also had a functioning replica built for his 1923 comedy film *Our Hospitality*, but its subsequent whereabouts are unknown.

Rocket really made it to the top of the celebrity tree when it appeared in animated form on TV in 2013 as Stephen (see what they did there?) in 'The Afternoon Tea Express' episode of *Thomas the Tank Engine and Friends*.

KERR, STUART TANK ENGINES

Designer:
Kerr, Stuart & Company
Built:
Stoke-on-Trent, Staffordshire; *c*.1890–1920
Railway:
Worldwide
Power:
Steam
Wheel arrangement:
From 0-4-0 up to 0-6-2
Main service life:
Worldwide
Current whereabouts:
Worldwide

Although Kerr, Stuart & Company did produce some larger locomotives for standard-gauge mainline service, what they really excelled at was building tough little narrow-gauge tank engines that went where other engines could not go, and did the jobs that other engines could not handle. They were, if you like, the tugboats of the railway world.

Tank engines were so called because they carried their own water tanks (and fuel bunkers), as opposed to having the huge tenders that bigger locomotives trailed behind to slake their thirst and feed their hungry fires over long distances. Kerr, Stuart made saddle-tank (so called because the water tank straddled the boiler) and side-tank (water tanks running alongside one or both sides of the boiler) locomotives, both of which proved so strong and reliable that they were soon in huge demand.

JOAN

Many of the tank engines are being or have been restored at museums and heritage railways around the world. Perhaps the most impressive of these is *Joan*, the 0-6-2T (side-tank engine) rescued from a disused sugar plantation in Antigua in 1971 and now back in working order on the Welshpool and Llanfair Railway in Wales.

In addition to the sterling industrial and passenger-carrying work they carried out all over Britain, here is a short sample of where else in the world these peripatetic little engines went to punch well above their weight:

ANTIGUA: transportation of cane from the sugar plantations to the mills dotted around the island

SOUTH AFRICA: provision of supplies to siege areas during the Second Boer War

FALKLAND ISLANDS: supply of coal to the generators of the Admiralty's wireless station

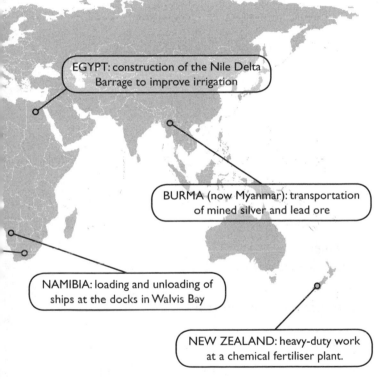

EGYPT: construction of the Nile Delta Barrage to improve irrigation

BURMA (now Myanmar): transportation of mined silver and lead ore

NAMIBIA: loading and unloading of ships at the docks in Walvis Bay

NEW ZEALAND: heavy-duty work at a chemical fertiliser plant.

FLYING SCOTSMAN

Designer:
Nigel Gresley
Built:
Doncaster, South Yorkshire; 1923
Railway:
LNER (London North Eastern Railway)
Power:
Steam
Class:
A1 (upgraded to A3 in 1947)
Wheel arrangement:
4-6-2 Pacific (plus 8-wheel tender)
Number:
4472
Maximum speed:
100 mph
Main service life:
London to Edinburgh
Current whereabouts:
National Railway Museum, York

Flying Scotsman was employed to pull long-distance express trains, including the 10 a.m. London to Edinburgh Flying Scotsman service, after which it was named. It was the first steam locomotive to break the 100-mph barrier, and holds the world record for the longest non-stop run by a steam locomotive (422 miles).

Having retired from normal service in 1963 after an active life of 2 million miles, it was rescued and lovingly restored by British businessman Alan Pegler (British Rail had wanted to scrap it for £3,000). It has since performed more farewell tours than U2 and the Rolling Stones put together, including the lengthy North American farewell tour (1969–73) and the Australian farewell tour (1988–89).

Coming under threat again in 2004, 6,500 individuals chipped in to save *Flying Scotsman* for the nation, with British entrepreneur Richard Branson matching their donations. It is expected that more farewell tours will follow its current 10-year overhaul at the National Railway Museum in York (where, it is rumoured, Bono and Mick Jagger are next in line for similar treatment).

The locomotive's celebrity appearances had, in fact, started as early as 1924, when it appeared at the British Empire Exhibition at Wembley, and it has also featured strongly in popular culture since the early days of its life:

1929: Starred in its own film, *The Flying Scotsman*, a thriller that included dangerous stunts. At one point, actress Pauline Johnson walks along the narrow outside ledge of the speeding train to get from the carriages to the locomotive – in high heels!

1968: Made a guest appearance in literary form as Gordon's brother in *Enterprising Engines*, the twenty-third book in the Reverend W. Awdry's *The Railway Series*.

1986: Appeared in a TV advert for British Rail, who clearly felt no shame about their earlier intentions to sell it for scrap.

2001: Entered the twenty-first century as one of the locomotives in the *Microsoft Train Simulator* game.

2012: Featured on one of the commemorative £5 coins minted for the London Olympics.

MALLARD

Designer:
Nigel Gresley
Built:
Doncaster, South Yorkshire; 1938
Railway:
LNER (London and North Eastern Railway)
Power:
Steam
Class:
A4
Wheel arrangement:
4-6-2 Pacific (plus 8-wheel tender)
Number:
4468
Maximum speed:
126 mph
Main service life:
Britain, East Coast Main Line
Current whereabouts:
National Railway Museum, York

Mallard was number 28 of 35 class A4 Pacifics built between 1935 and 1938. Designer Nigel Gresley was a keen birdwatcher and named most of the locomotives after birds. He made exceptions at the outset, though, naming the first four locomotives Silver Link, Quicksilver, Silver King and Silver Fox, just to keep George V happy in his silver jubilee year (1935). You might argue that a mallard was one of the less exciting birds to be used in the naming process (others included golden eagle, falcon and peregrine), but this duck proved to be anything but lame when it came to performance.

Its Bugatti-style streamlined shape, developed in wind-tunnel tests, lowered wind resistance and drew smoke away from the cab. It broke the world speed record for a steam locomotive on 3 July 1938, heading south at 125.88 mph near Grantham in Lincolnshire, a record it holds to this day. It looked the part as well, especially in its spruced-up post-war livery of garter blue with red and white lining.

It served its time on the East Coast Line, gracing the Yorkshire Pullman and Flying Scotsman services with its presence and power, and was finally retired in 1963. It is now prominently displayed in the Great Hall of the National Railway Museum in York. On the cultural front, it achieved some additional cult status when it appeared on the cover of Britpop band Blur's 1993 album *Modern Life is Rubbish*.

DUCHESS OF HAMILTON

Designer:
William Stanier
Built:
Crewe, Lancashire; 1938
Railway:
LMS (London, Midland and Scottish Railway)
Power:
Steam
Class:
Princess Coronation
Wheel arrangement:
4-6-2 Pacific (plus 6-wheel tender)
Number:
6229
Maximum speed:
114 mph
Main service life:
Britain, West Coast Main Line
Current whereabouts:
National Railway Museum, York

Nigel Gresley didn't have it all his own way at LNER. While he was taking plaudits for the likes of *Mallard* running up and down the East Coast Main Line of Britain, his contemporary rival, William

Stanier, was doing the same thing over on the West Coast Main Line. Stanier's triumphs included the Princess Coronation Class, the most powerful (3,300 horsepower) passenger steam locomotive ever built. The *Duchess of Hamilton* was one of the few of that class to be streamlined, i.e. styled a lot like Gresley's *Mallard*, but Stanier took that step only under sufferance. Born in Swindon, Wiltshire, to a father who worked for the Great Western Railway, he preferred a no-nonsense approach to design and liked his locomotives to look like locomotives.

The streamlining was later removed from the *Duchess* and, after being taken out of service, she spent a period of ignominy as an exhibit at a Billy Butlin's Holiday Camp. Following a recent restoration, however, she now sits in the National Railway Museum in all her original streamlined glory, and right alongside *Mallard* at that. Just don't tell William Stanier.

20TH CENTURY LIMITED HUDSONS

Designer
Paul W. Kiefer
Built:
Schenectady, New York; 1927–38

Railway:
New York Central Railroad
Power:
Steam
Class:
J-1, J-2, J-3
Wheel arrangement:
4-6-4 Hudson (plus 12-wheel tender)
Maximum speed:
100 mph
Main service life:
New York to Chicago
Current whereabouts:
All scrapped

North American trains, from the early steam locomotives to the powerful diesels that replaced them, have always been massive and muscular. Once US train designers added streamlining and a large dose of the art-deco style so popular in the interwar years of the twentieth century, they started to look decidedly space age as well. From the cross-country Chiefs and Super Chiefs of the Atchison, Topeka and Santa Fe Railway to the Zephyrs of the Chicago, Burlington and Quincy Railroad, they most certainly looked the part.

The most famous train of all was the New York Central Railroad's 20th Century Limited service, which ran along the Hudson Valley between New York and Chicago from 1902 until 1967, and which was for decades referred to as 'the greatest train in the world', at least by the American press.

Powered for a long time by the iconic Hudson locomotives built by Alco (American Locomotive Company), passengers walked along a red carpet to board its equally iconic Pullman carriages. In 1934 the train became even more famous when it starred in a film also named after it, the screwball comedy *20th Century*, starring John Barrymore and Carole Lombard.

In the 1940s the Alco steam locomotives were replaced by General Motors E7 'bulldog-nosed' diesels, and in this incarnation the train landed another big role, this time in the 1959 Alfred Hitchcock spy thriller *North by Northwest*, starring Cary Grant as 'regular guy on train mistaken for spy'.

UNION PACIFIC BIG BOY

Designer:
Otto Jabelmann
Built:
Schenectady, New York; 1941–44

Railway:
Union Pacific Railroad
Power:
Steam
Class:
4000
Wheel arrangement
4-8-8-4 (plus 14-wheel tender)
Maximum speed:
80 mph
Main service life:
Green River, Wyoming to Ogden, Utah
Current whereabouts:
Various US museums

The 7,000-horsepower Big Boys made by Alco (American Locomotive Company) for the Union Pacific Railroad hauled mile-long freight trains for 20 years over the Wasatch Mountains between Wyoming and Utah, each one notching up over a million miles in the process. They also provided valuable support during World War Two by hauling huge numbers of troops, raw materials and military equipment around the country.

At 40 metres long from the cowcatcher at the front to the tender that carried 114,000 litres of water and 26,000 tons of coal at the back, each locomotive weighed as much as a hundred elephants (400 tons). The driving wheels alone were each 1.73 metres in diameter. If you want to feel really small, go and stand next to one of the eight that remain in railroad museums dotted around the USA (only 25 were ever made). Union Pacific has plans to restore one of the engines to operating condition at its steam shop in Cheyenne, Wyoming.

TGV

Designer:
GEC-Alsthom (now Alstom)
Built:
France (initially), 1970s onwards
Railway:
SNCF (Société Nationale des Chemins de Fer Français)
Power:
Overhead electric
Maximum speed:
357 mph
Main service life:
High-speed French and international routes
Current whereabouts:
Worldwide

French train builders used to let it all hang out, leaving their trains looking like Pompidou Centres on wheels, and perhaps this was one of the reasons they couldn't wait to get rid of steam once a sleek electric alternative became available in the 1970s. The Train à Grande Vitesse (TGV) they came up with, however, was way beyond a simple upgrade of their previous efforts, going on to revolutionise rail travel the world over. Since the very first one went into service in 1981, TGVs have been the gold standard for high-speed rail travel. Here are just a few of the TGV's achievements:

➤ The first train in Europe to be scheduled to run at 200 km/h (124 mph).

➤ Holder of the world speed record for conventional trains (357 mph) since 2007.

➤ For many years TGVs produced the fastest average start-to-stop speed of any scheduled service (*c*.175 mph).

➤ Broke the world speed record for an international journey when a Eurostar TGV carried the cast and producers of *The Da Vinci Code* from London to Cannes for the eponymous film festival in 2006. It covered the 883 miles in 7 hours 25 minutes.

There are now well over 500 TGVs in France alone, including a double-decker version. Other countries have adopted the technology and now run their own models, such that TGVs can be admired across continental Europe and in parts of Asia and the Americas.

SHINKANSEN SERIES 0

Designer:
Hideo Shima
Built:
Japan; 1963–86
Railway:
Japanese National Railways
Power:
Overhead electric
Class:
Series 0
Maximum speed:
170 mph
Main service life:
Tokyo to Osaka (initially)
Current whereabouts:
Various Japanese museums

Launched in 1964 in time for the Tokyo Olympics that year, the Shinkansen (meaning 'new trunk line') led the way in high-speed rail travel. Its revolutionary features included power to every single wheel axle, automatic braking, an in-cab track-signalling system, double-glazing, air conditioning and on-board telephones. Trains ran on new, dedicated tracks and, on average, arrived within 24 seconds of their schedule. The Shinkansen was dubbed the 'bullet train' because of its streamlined appearance and rounded nose, as well as its then record-breaking speed of 170 mph.

Subsequent series of the Shinkansen might make the Series 0 look slow by comparison, but it will forever sit in the record books as the world's first superfast train. A total of 3,216 entered service, and the last one wasn't retired until 2008. Twenty-six of the trains are preserved in various Japanese museums, and there is also one in Britain, at the National Railway Museum in York.

SHANGHAI MAGLEV

Designer:
Transrapid International
Built:
Kassell, Germany; 1963
Railway:
Chinese National Railways

Power:
Magnetic levitation
Maximum speed:
311 mph
Main service life:
Shanghai Airport to Shanghai Metro line
Current whereabouts:
Shanghai Airport to Shanghai Metro line

The Shanghai Maglev is the fastest train line in the world and was the first commercial service to operate by magnetic levitation at high speed. The German-built Transrapid 09 trains wrap their 'arms' under a T-shaped 'monorail' to achieve forward propulsion and levitation through magnetic force alone. It is the first time in the history of rail travel that trains can run without making contact with their track. It takes less than 2 minutes for the 'floating bullet' trains to reach 200 mph, with their 19-mile journey between Shanghai Pudong International Airport and the Longyang Road metro station taking a mere 7 minutes 20 seconds.

Whether maglev technology is the future of rail travel depends on whether business cases can justify the huge investment required to travel even faster than the already superfast 'traditional' high-speed electric trains that continue to spread around the world. It is a very expensive toy, but also a very impressive one.

PULLMAN CARRIAGES

Designer:
George Pullman
Built:
USA; 1863 onwards
Railway:
Most US railroads (initially)
Main service life:
US railroads and international Orient Express services
Current whereabouts:
Worldwide

I know a Pullman carriage can't go anywhere on its own, but I think it deserves a place in the train hall of fame on account of its longstanding reputation for providing rail travel at the sheer luxury end of the scale.

In 1865 industrialist George Pullman loaned the US government one of his recently built luxury sleeping cars as part of the cortege that conveyed the body of assassinated president Abraham Lincoln from Washington, D.C. to his burial place at Springfield, Illinois. It proved to be a stroke of marketing genius as the millions who lined the route to pay their respects to Lincoln over a 2-week period were also treated to their first glimpse of luxury rail travel. Orders flooded in from rail companies and the cars were thereafter named in Pullman's honour, becoming synonymous with the 'luxury hotel on wheels' status later enjoyed by the likes of the Orient Express.

No expense was spared and only the finest crystal, silver, mahogany, black walnut and marble were considered good enough to meet the sleeping, observing and fine-dining needs of those passengers with enough money or prestige not to have to travel with ordinary folk, who, after all, could probably not be relied upon to dress properly for dinner. Service was always impeccable, and recruitment was never a problem in the early days when the market was awash with recently freed house slaves.

The carriages have starred in their own right in countless books and films, as apt settings for high-end spies like James Bond and high-end detectives like Hercule Poirot. They have also starred in real life as the bedrooms, offices and dining cars of the world's royal families, presidents, maharajas, spies and celebrities. The *Ferdinand Magellan* Pullman carriage that transported the US president was, between 1943 and 1958, the armour-plated, bullet-resistant, US-railroad equivalent of the Air Force One presidential plane.

WHAT'S IN A NAME?

We have seen how many individual locomotives and services were given personalised names. This was usually done for marketing purposes and also sometimes to give train builders and railway employees a sense that their trains 'belonged' to them. Naming conventions have been random affairs, different designers and railway companies each doing their own thing for each class of locomotive or each route. Locomotive names have been adopted from worthy subjects as wide-ranging as military regiments, commanders and battles, literature, royalty, animals, castles and stately homes, ships, planes, countries and cities, mythological creatures, planets, birds and many more besides. In fact, it's probably the only thing that Robin Hood, Yuri Gagarin and the Duchess of Hamilton have in common. Just occasionally, though, trains or routes have been given names that are a little more unusual or frivolous than the norm:

The Lunatic Express: the railway system that linked the interiors of Uganda and Kenya to the Indian Ocean. Completed in 1902, it gained the name on account of the dangerous working conditions of those who built it, which included tropical diseases, hostile tribes and the infamous man-eating lions of Tsavo, which pulled railway workers out of their carriages at night.

———————

The Fish and **The Chips:** two complementary commuter services that run over the Blue Mountains between Sydney and Lithgow in Australia.

———————

Thunderbirds: the fleet of Virgin trains used to rescue broken-down locomotives are all named after Thunderbirds characters: Brains, Virgil Tracy, Lady Penelope, Parker, etc. All nameplates are blue, except, of course, for the one displayed on the *Lady Penelope*.

JUMBO TRAIN

The longest, heaviest train ever recorded stretched out for more than 4.5 miles and weighed 95,000 tonnes, the equivalent of 27,000 fully grown elephants. The freight train consisted of eight diesel locomotives hauling 682 wagons loaded with iron ore over a distance of 175 miles to the huge harbour at Port Hedland in Western Australia. You didn't want to get stuck at the level crossing that day.

ICONIC RAILWAY STATIONS

The only way to be sure of catching a train is to miss the one before it.

G. K. Chesterton

The French government obviously didn't agree with English writer G. K. Chesterton, because, in 1891, they ordered all clocks inside stations to run 5 minutes later than standard Paris Mean Time. In this way, they meant to increase the number of passengers catching their train without missing the previous one. I am not sure if it worked, but the system remained in place until 1911.

Fellow English writer E. M. Forster definitely got it spot on, though, because railway stations, and railway terminals in particular, remain our gateways to the major cities of the world and to many other destinations besides.

As gateways go, the great railway stations are some of the engineering and architectural wonders of the modern age. From the early cathedrals and temples to the railway gods, often built in Classical or Gothic style, to the aesthetically inspiring modernity of today's builds and rebuilds, many of them rank amongst the most beautiful buildings in the world. They are also amongst the most functional of the world's buildings, often serving simultaneously as transport arteries, shopping malls, bookstores and eateries catering to every taste.

Some railway stations are also iconic for reasons of history or geography, or for having served as admirable settings for important literature and films.

Whatever the reason for their iconic status in our consciousness, we will look at a few of the most significant ones in this chapter.

ST PANCRAS INTERNATIONAL

Location: London, England
Opened: 1868 (rebuilt 2007)
Designer: William Henry Barlow (1868); Alastair Lansley (2007)

 Barlow's pointed-arch train shed was a daring single span of iron and glass, at the time the largest of its kind in the world. It reached a height of 30 metres and a width of 73 metres, the height being needed for steam trains to let off steam and smoke without choking everybody in the station to death. This was one of the main reasons that Barlow's design was subsequently copied around the world.

In 1873 the Midland Grand Hotel (now the St Pancras Renaissance), designed by architect George Gilbert Scott, was added as a Victorian-Gothic-Revival-style frontispiece to the station and has been a love-it-or-hate-it London landmark ever since.

The station escaped a planned demolition in the 1960s, not least thanks to English poet Sir John Betjeman, a driving force behind the campaign mounted to save its original fabric and design. By 2007 the station had not just been saved and sympathetically renovated, it had been expanded to become the quite stunning modern hub for Eurostar services to France and Belgium, thereby gaining its international suffix. A wonderful lifelike statue of Betjeman by sculptor Martin Jennings stands in the international terminal as a fitting tribute to the poet's efforts.

In 2012 the station also served as the terminus for the Olympic Javelin service, a 7-minute shuttle between Central London and the Olympic Park.

THE UNDOUBTED MAGIC OF KING'S CROSS

Adjoining St Pancras International is London King's Cross Station, gateway to the East Coast Main Line and erstwhile launch pad for the likes of *Flying Scotsman* and *Mallard*. It, too, has enjoyed a recent makeover, including a magnificent new roof engineered by the Arup Group that has been described as a 'reverse waterfall'. Perhaps it is appropriate, then, that the station also houses Platform 9¾, the magical gateway to the Hogwarts Express.

A special Platform 9¾ sign, complete with luggage trolley embedded in a brick wall, has recently been moved away from the platforms to the concourse area at King's Cross so that fans can queue for their photo opportunity without getting in the way of commuters who want to travel in a more conventional manner.

J. K. Rowling even set the epilogue to *Harry Potter and the Deathly Hallows* at King's Cross Station, giving it the undoubted honour of being the final setting in the whole series of Harry Potter books. That's what you call fame.

PLEASE LOOK AFTER THIS BEAR. THANK YOU.

London Paddington Station contains solemn statues of Isambard Kingdom Brunel, the man who built the Great Western Railway (GWR) and the station that was built to serve it, and a World War One 'Tommy' on the war memorial to the GWR employees who fell in that war.

The railway powers that be also showed they had a sense of humour when in 2000 they erected a statue of Paddington Bear in the station. The fictional bear created by Michael Bond in 1958 had, of course, been given the name 'Paddington' by the Brown family who found him at the station, just after he had arrived as a stowaway from deepest, darkest Peru, with the notice 'Please look after this bear' attached to his duffel coat.

CHHATRAPATI SHIVAJI TERMINUS

Location: Mumbai, India
Opened: 1888
Designer: Frederick William Stevens

Chhatrapati Shivaji started life as the Victoria Terminus in what was then Bombay in the year following the Golden Jubilee of Queen Victoria, the ruling monarch of the United Kingdom and, of course, the Empress of India. Awash with domes, turrets, stone carvings and pointed arches built in yellow sandstone, granite and blue-grey basalt, it paid homage to George Gilbert Scott's hotel at St Pancras, but the Gothic Revival style was complemented by Mughal influences, an ensemble intended to capture a unique coming together of western and eastern styles. The red double-decker buses and Hindustan Ambassador taxis (based on the 1954 Morris Oxford) that stream past it to this day only add to the general air of nostalgia. Quite fittingly, the station has been listed since 2004 as a UNESCO World Heritage Site.

As soon as you step inside, however, you realise that this is no bygone relic. Used by more than 3 million commuters a day, and colour-splashed by a sea of saris, it is one of the great stations in which to stand still. It is also as good place as any to hop on board and enjoy the unforgettable experience of a journey on Indian Railways.

The station has often appeared on screen, and in recent years starred as a major setting for *Slumdog Millionaire*, the 2008 Oscar-winning film directed by Englishman Danny Boyle.

ESTACIÓN DE ATOCHA

Location: Madrid, Spain
Opened: 1851 (rebuilt 1892 and 1992)
Designers: Alberto Palacio (1892), Rafael Moneo (1992)

After a fire had pretty much destroyed the original building, in 1892 Alberto Palacio adopted a style that made extensive use of wrought iron. He involved Frenchman Gustave Eiffel in the project, because apparently Monsieur Eiffel had some recent experience of his own in the building of a wrought-iron structure.

Exactly 100 years after the Palacio rebuild, the station then received the modern makeover that we see today, partly to accommodate Spain's growing high-speed rail network, and partly because it was time to get ready for the twenty-first century. Inside today's station (designed by Rafael Moneo), the original concourse has become a vast plaza filled with tropical plants and flowers and ponds full of goldfish and rare turtles, as well as housing a shopping mall and a nightclub.

Atocha (named after the nearby basilica dedicated to Our Lady of Atocha) is like a beating heart that serves the national and international arteries that flow out from it day after day in all directions.

GARE DU NORD

Location: Paris, France
Opened: 1846
Designer: Jacques Hittorff

Serving northern France, Belgium, the Netherlands, Germany and Britain, the Gare du Nord is by far the busiest railway station in Europe, and the busiest in the world outside Japan. It is also one of the world's oldest stations, dating from the very early days of the railway. For that reason, it seems to have undergone a fairly constant expansion programme throughout its history. As the arrival point today of Eurostar trains from London (for which another extension was undertaken in 1994), the station has become very familiar to millions of British business and leisure travellers.

The station, built in the Beaux Arts style, includes a huge 'triumphal arch' facade displaying 23 female statues, each representing a destination served by the station. They include allegorical representations of Berlin, Warsaw, Amsterdam, Vienna, Brussels and Frankfurt, with the figure representing Paris taking pride of place at the very top.

The Gare du Nord's screen appearances have included three blockbuster films already this century: action spy thriller *The Bourne Identity* (2002, Doug Liman), comedy heist *Ocean's Twelve* (2004, Steven Soderbergh), and the Bourne trilogy finale *The Bourne Ultimatum* (2007, Paul Greengrass).

GARE DE LYON

Location: Paris, France
Opened: 1900
Designer: Marius Toudoire

Built for the Exposition Universelle (World's Fair) held in Paris in 1900, the Gare de Lyon was a *fin-de-siècle* triumph of belle époque sculpture and paintings. In addition to handling the increased capacity needed to support the fair, the station became a glorious setting for the arrival and departure of *Le Train Bleu*, the renowned service that carried the rich and famous to and from the French Riviera. The interior of the station is best known for the restaurant that bears the name of, and pays homage to, *Le Train Bleu*. Here, budget permitting, you can be fine-wined and dined while admiring the 30 scenes (by 30 different artists) of towns served by the erstwhile PLM (Paris–Lyon–Marseilles Railway).

Times inside the restaurant have not changed much in over a hundred years but outside is a different matter, to the extent that nowadays you could reach the Riviera on a high-speed train in about the same time as you might spend on a leisurely lunch while not giving a single thought to the world outside.

The station's screen roles have included the 2006 British ITV adaptation of the Agatha Christie thriller *The Mystery of the Blue Train*, and the 2010 film *The Tourist* (Florian Henckel von Donnersmarck), a romantic comedy thriller starring Johnny Depp and Angelina Jolie.

WHEN IS A RAILWAY STATION NOT A RAILWAY STATION?

The Gare d'Orsay in Paris, built in the Beaux Arts style in 1900 but rendered largely redundant by 1939 on account of its short platforms, reopened in 1986 as a stunning art museum, the Musée d'Orsay. It houses the largest collection of impressionist and post-impressionist masterpieces in the world, including works by Monet, Manet, van Gogh, Gauguin and Renoir. One of the finest views in Paris today is looking out from the top level of the museum through one of the former station's two giant clocks, across the Seine to Sacré-Cœur in the north of the city.

MON DIEU! LA LOCOMOTIVE EST DANS LA PLACE

On 22 October 1895, an express steam train from Granville in Normandy arrived at Gare Montparnasse in Paris. Unfortunately, it didn't stop there. Smashing through the buffers and across the concourse, it exited through a large first-floor window and ended up nose-first on the square below the station. Fortunately, the passenger carriages remained within the station. The photographs taken of the 'hanging' locomotive have been widely reproduced, and a replica of the scene has even been built at a theme park in Brazil.

GRAND CENTRAL TERMINAL

Location: New York City, NY
Opened: 1913
Designers: Reed and Stem (overall design); Warren and Wetmore (Beaux Arts style)

Built in the Beaux Arts style, Grand Central features a massive marbled staircase, a huge, blue-green astronomical painting on the main concourse ceiling, a facade sporting many classical statues (perhaps influenced by the style of the Gare du Nord in Paris) and a giant Tiffany clock, and the famous four-faced clock that serves as a meeting point inside. The station survived a demolition threat in the 1960s, with former First Lady Jacqueline Kennedy influential in getting the building designated a US National Historic Landmark.

With more platforms than any other station in the world (44), it has been said of Grand Central that you could spend hours there without ever getting bored, even if you had nowhere to travel to. Work up an appetite by wandering around the myriad shops or food market, try a cocktail at the smart Campbell Apartment, follow that with some oysters at the Grand Central Oyster Bar, then move on to a juicy steak at Michael Jordan's Steak House. If you're on a budget, have some free fun instead at the whispering gallery on the dining concourse, where low, ceramic arches will carry your whispered sayings around the dome of the curved ceiling as if you had almost shouted them.

Even if you haven't been to Grand Central, you probably think you have because, like so many Manhattan landmarks, the station has been appearing on your television and cinema screens since forever. The many Hollywood movies to have been filmed there include crime drama *Carlito's Way* (1993, Brian de Palma), sci-fi action comedy *Men in Black* (1997, Barry Sonnenfeld), tragic drama *Revolutionary Road* (2008, Sam Mendes) and superhero film *The Avengers* (2012, Joss Whedon). Such saturated screen coverage probably accounts for the fact that Grand Central is one of the most-visited tourist attractions in the world, and most of those tourists never get on a train.

UNION STATION, WASHINGTON

 Location: Washington, DC
Opened: 1907 (renovated 1988)
Designer: Daniel Burnham (renovation by Benjamin Thompson Associates)

The world's biggest station when it opened (if you laid the Washington Monument on its side, it would fit inside), Union Station housed a Turkish bath, a bowling alley and a mortuary. It was a masterpiece of the Beaux Arts style, modelled on the Arch of Constantine and the Caracalla Baths in Rome, a fitting setting for the several presidential inauguration balls to have been held there. A 1988 renovation was respectful of the original style but also reflected the cultural changes that had taken place in the USA since 1907, with parking for 1,500 cars, a nine-screen cinema and a multitude of cafes, bars, restaurants and shops taking the place of the Turkish bath, bowling alley and mortuary.

UNION STATION, LOS ANGELES

Location: Los Angeles, California
Opened: 1939
Designer: John and Donald Parkinson (father and son)

The 'Spanish Colonial Art Deco' style of this station exudes an almost spiritual air, its white bell tower reminiscent of California's mission halls. Set within beautifully landscaped gardens and cool courtyards, there can be few more relaxing spaces in which to await a train. Terracotta, marble and steel were all made use of to keep passengers cool in this refuge from the fierce Californian sun. Built to host the great trains of the Southern Pacific, Union Pacific and Santa Fe railroads, the station will be known in future as much for the part it plays as a hub in the California High-Speed Rail Link.

Not surprisingly, given its proximity to Hollywood, the station has been used as a setting in scores of movies, including romantic drama *The Way We Were* (1973, Sydney Pollack), comedy thriller *Silver Streak* (Arthur Hiller, 1976), sci-fi thriller *Blade Runner* (Ridley Scott, 1982) and war epic *Pearl Harbor* (Michael Bay, 2001).

BERLIN HAUPTBAHNHOF

Location: Berlin, Germany
Opened: 2006
Designer: Meinhard von Gerkan

After the Berlin Wall came down in 1989, Germany set about reconnecting its rail network and chose the site of the old Lehrter Bahnhof in Berlin to be developed as the hub. When the striking Berlin Hauptbahnhof finally opened in 2006, it was hailed as an architectural wonder and a proud symbol of east/west reunification. Perhaps somewhat bizarrely in the political circumstances, the architects adopted what they described as French Renaissance style, but I have to say that the colossal steel and glass structure strikes me as more twenty-first century than medieval château.

The station is also something of an engineering triumph, involving a number of perpendicular levels, the highest at 10 metres above ground and the lowest at 15 metres below, with a diversion of the River Spree thrown in for good measure. Tracks run on two of the levels, handling up to 1,800 trains and 350,000 passengers each day.

HELSINKI CENTRAL

Location: Helsinki, Finland
Opened: 1918
Designer: Eliel Saarinen

With independence from Soviet Russia in the air, and the music of Jean Sibelius in full flow, Finnish architects enjoyed a hitherto unimaginable freedom of expression in the early twentieth century. Nowhere is this more evident than in Saarinen's station, arguably the Finnish capital city's most striking landmark. Two pairs of giant lantern-bearing statues, one pair on either side of the main entrance, dominate its granite-clad facade and look especially impressive when the huge spherical lanterns are lit at night. Along with an equally huge clock tower, they positively loom over the surrounding area.

The station continues to impress today. Trains run on time, the food and service within is good, and the building is spotlessly clean. Over 200,000 passengers a day make it the country's most-visited building.

KAZANSKY

 Location: Moscow, Russia
Opened: 1864 (rebuilt by 1926)
Designer: Alexey Shchusev

The citadel-style Kazansky Station sits on Komsomolskaya Square, along with Leningradsky and Yaroslavsky Stations. Trains from here serve Kazan (Russian terminals are generally named after the cities their trains travel to), and Shchusev's rebuild was modelled on the Söyembikä Tower within that city's kremlin. You can also begin a Trans-Siberian journey here, but not before enjoying some food and a vodka or five under the gloriously over-the-top ceiling of the station restaurant – it would not look out of place at the Bolshoi.

STESEN KERETAPI KUALA LUMPUR

Location: Kuala Lumpur, Malaysia
Opened: 1910
Designer: Brigadier General Arthur Benison Hubback

You could be forgiven for missing this station entirely (and I did, at least initially) because, from the outside, it looks more like a Raj-style pavilion than a railway station. Apparently, at the time it was built, that well-known mixture of Neo-Moorish/Mughal/Indo-Saracenic (think lots of arches and minaret-like domes) with the odd dollop of western influence was all the rage.

After a lot of its traffic was moved to nearby Kuala Lumpur Sentral, much of the station was converted to a railway museum in 2007, with many of the original station's furnishings now set within the on-site Heritage Station Hotel.

KANAZAWA

Location: Ishikawa Province, Honshu Island, Japan
Opened: 1898 (rebuilt in the 1990s)

Entirely elevated above street level, the futuristic architecture of Kanazawa Station includes the Montenashi (Welcome) Dome, which resembles a huge glass umbrella, and the equally huge Tsuzumi-mon, a wooden 'temple shrine' gateway that symbolises traditional Japanese hand drums (tsuzumis). Outside is a fountain that changes its flow pattern so as always to digitally display the current time. The recent addition of a Shinkansen (bullet train) link, which puts the city within 2 hours 30 minutes of Tokyo, has further helped to put Kanazawa firmly on the Japanese railway map.

ANTWERPEN-CENTRAAL

Location: Antwerp, Belgium
Opened: 1905
Designer: Louis Delacenserie/Clement van Bogaert

If you like neo-Baroque palaces, try Antwerpen-Centraal. Nicknamed the 'Railway Cathedral' on account of its huge size, iron-and-glass vaulted ceiling and over-the-top interior, it was kitted out with 20 different kinds of marble and stone. An award-winning reconstruction in the early part of this century has converted what was previously a terminus to a through-station on three separate levels, but without losing any of the original splendour. Often voted one of the most beautiful stations in the world, it went viral in 2009 when a flash mob of 200 dancers of all ages staged a choreographed performance of 'Do-Re-Mi' from *The Sound of Music* to advertise a Belgian TV talent show, *Op zoek naar Maria*, their version of the BBC talent show *How Do You Solve a Problem Like Maria?*

HUA HIN

Location: Hua Hin, Thailand
Opened: 1922

One of Thailand's oldest, Hua Hin Station was built to allow the king and his family access to their nearby summer palace. The little pavilion-like station is a photographer's paradise on account of its exotic architecture and colourful people-watching opportunities. The Royal Waiting Room looks particularly delicate, which isn't surprising seeing as it started life as a royal pavilion in the grounds of Sanam Chandra Palace at Nakhon Pathom before being moved to the station in 1968 to allow the royal family to feel at home while they were waiting to go home. Train enthusiasts can also enjoy the retired US-built 2-8-2 Mikado steam locomotive that is housed at the station, and even on the odd occasion admire the Eastern & Oriental Express as it passes through on its way from Bangkok to Kuala Lumpur and Singapore.

VENEZIA SANTA LUCIA

Location: Venice, Italy
Opened: 1861 (with 1952 rebuild)
Designers: Angiolo Mazzoni/Virgilio Vallot/Paul Perilli (1952 rebuild)

State architect Mazzoni first planned the current station in 1924 but, in true Italian fashion, it took three architects, countless designs and redesigns, and almost 30 years to complete. It is one of the few Modernist buildings to overlook the Grand Canal, which means that train passengers spill straight out of the station on to one of the wonders of the world, having crossed the Ponte della Libertà, the 2-mile causeway from the mainland, only moments before. Location, location, location!

Whether you set out from London on the Orient Express, or from Milan on a high-speed train, or from a local station across on the mainland, there are not many train journeys that deliver you straight into the heart of a completely different world to that which you left behind. 'Just add water' is perhaps what it should say on the train ticket.

BRITISH BY DESIGN

Keeping alive a long British tradition that started with Brunel's groundbreaking nineteenth-century design for London Paddington, British architect Norman Foster has in more recent times designed a new roof for Dresden Hauptbahnhof in Germany, a new high-speed rail terminus in Florence, Italy, the Canary Wharf station on the London Underground, and four stations on the Mecca–Medina high-speed line in Saudi Arabia.

EELS AND ANTS

If you want a wonderful bird's-eye view of a railway station, book up for the view from the Shard, one of London's newest and most iconic skyscrapers. You will be able to gaze down on what look like lots of eels slithering in and out of London Bridge Station far below, and marvel at the thousands of ants that the eels seem to disgorge upon arrival, before gorging on lots more before setting off again.

You will also be able to see how progress is going on the rebuilding project that will bring London's oldest station bang into the twenty-first century, including a single concourse serving all 15 platforms that will be bigger than the football pitch at Wembley Stadium.

GREAT RAILWAY JOURNEYS

There's something about the sound of a train that's very romantic and nostalgic and hopeful.

Paul Simon

It was while waiting in a railway station, with a ticket to his destination, that Paul Simon penned the lyrics in 1964 for 'Homeward Bound', Simon and Garfunkel's second hit song. The railway station in question was Widnes, Lancashire and the train he was waiting for was the early-morning milk train down to London, which was indeed his home at that time. The Widnes to London milk train was probably never one of the world's great railway journeys, but that particular journey was for Simon more about the destination than the journey. There are, however, many railway journeys that are worth doing as much for the journey as the destination.

Great railway journeys abound the world over, and always will. They afford the opportunity to travel on trains of all shapes and sizes and ages, from those driven by steam to those propelled by magnetic levitation. They cover their respective territories on track gauges suitable to their terrain, whether pastoral or desert, or through mountains or across or under water. What makes a railway journey great is a matter of subjective opinion, and it would be impossible to cover them all in anything less than an encyclopaedia, so I will do what everyone else does and select a number of personal favourites, some of which I have already enjoyed, the rest of which remain firmly on my bucket list.

But let us start by paying homage to the two men who first recognised the greatness of the railway journey, who first alerted the world to its very many possibilities: George Bradshaw and Thomas Cook.

NOW, THAT'S WHAT YOU CALL A RAILWAY GUIDE, BY GEORGE!

Lancashire-born George Bradshaw produced the world's first compilation of railway timetables in 1839. As the railways of Britain and Europe grew, so did the publications of his timetables and travel guides to service the burgeoning tourism industry. Their reach ultimately extended further east to include, by 1903, the magnificently titled *Bradshaw's Through Routes to the Capitals of the World, and Overland Guide to India, Persia and the Far East*. Bradshaw had died prematurely of cholera in 1853 at the age of 52, but the books that bore his name continued until 1961.

His name became synonymous with rail travel, to the extent that travellers referred to their 'Bradshaw' as opposed to their 'timetable', in the same way that people often still refer to their 'Hoover' as opposed to their 'vacuum cleaner'. He even made it as a verb during World War Two when 'to Bradshaw' meant to navigate an aeroplane along the course of a railway line below.

Although current Bradshaw's guides are no longer available to us as we plan our own great railway journeys, the reproductions that we can buy today of some of the old ones remain a fascinating account of a bygone age, with some descriptions that might take you by surprise if you were to see them in a guidebook today:

Hastings (East Sussex):
A very efficient substitute for a trip to Madeira.

Hull (East Yorkshire):
Seems to rise like Venice from amidst the sea.

'COOK'S TOURS'

Englishman Thomas Cook was a former Baptist minister who had taken the no-alcohol pledge and set about encouraging others to do the same. In 1841 he arranged a rail excursion for 540 travellers to attend a temperance rally, convincing the railway company that each should be charged a flat fee including the cost of their food on the day. Encouraged by his success, he set about arranging rail excursions for pleasure, and the package deal was born. Once he could no longer cope with going along as guide on every package holiday he arranged, he came up with the idea of inclusive independent travel, setting his clients up with all the bookings, documents and information they needed to travel the world's railways (and steamers) by themselves. The concept of visiting a number of destinations according to a single itinerary within a confined amount of time became popularly known as a 'Cook's Tour'.

THE MAN IN SEAT SIXTY-ONE

Our twenty-first-century version of George Bradshaw's guides is this travel website (www.seat61. com), which focuses almost entirely on train-based travel around the world. It is run by Englishman Mark Smith, an ex rail-industry manager, and has won numerous awards for its advice about the best routes, times and costs for travelling from just about anywhere to just about anywhere else. The name of the website derives from his own favourite seat when travelling first class to Europe on Eurostar, as do the accompanying books based on his own travels.

Starting in the Scottish Highlands, and finishing at Machu Picchu, let us now have a look at just some of the great railway journeys available to us today. George Bradshaw and Thomas Cook would have loved them all. The Man in Seat Sixty-One still does.

WEST HIGHLAND LINE (SCOTLAND)

Not just generally accepted to be the most scenic railway journey in Britain, the West Highland Line is also regularly voted the best railway journey in the world. If you are setting out from London, the first part of your journey will be to Fort William, at the foot of Ben Nevis in the Scottish Highlands, on the 9 p.m. scheduled Caledonian Sleeper (every night of the year except Saturdays). Enjoy haggis, neeps and tatties washed down with a malt or two from the on-board bar before retiring to dream of the scenery that will greet you over breakfast.

An extension of the West Highland Line takes you out west from Fort William to Mallaig, opposite the Isle of Skye. The three options for travelling this route are the run-of-the-mill scheduled service, the Jacobite steam service that runs in the summer and has in recent years been immortalised as the Hogwarts Express in the Harry Potter films, and the luxurious Royal Scotsman service, which runs Highland tours in the summer out of Edinburgh. Mile for mile, the Royal Scotsman is the most expensive railway service in the world and you will need to dress in your stateroom for dinner while agonising over which of the 30 malt whiskies to try next. Whether you blow your savings on the Royal Scotsman or take the local train, the scenery will be the same: mile after mile of spectacular mountains, lochs and deer-filled glens.

GLENFINNAN VIADUCT

Known to millions of Harry Potter fans as the viaduct that the Hogwarts Express winds across, the Glenfinnan Viaduct is an engineering wonder built in 1898 by 'Concrete Bob' (Sir Robert McAlpine) at a time when poured-concrete construction was positively revolutionary. Spanning 380 metres, the 21 semi-circular arches reach a height of 30 metres, offering rail passengers quite spectacular views of Loch Shiel and beyond. In recognition of McAlpine's genius, the viaduct is depicted on the back of a Bank of Scotland £10 note. The Harry Potter production team based for nine years, on and off, in the tiny village of Glenfinnan must have got through a few of them.

SETTLE–CARLISLE LINE (ENGLAND)

This 72-mile line between Settle in North Yorkshire and Carlisle in Cumbria offers wonderful views as it takes in the more remote moors of the Yorkshire Dales, one of England's National Parks, and the North Pennines, a designated Area of Outstanding Natural Beauty.

The terrain was difficult to build through when the line was constructed in the nineteenth century, and 14 tunnels and 21 glorious viaducts, including the longest at Ribblehead and the highest at Smardale, were needed to cross the moors and cut through the Pennines. Dent Station in Cumbria is the highest mainline station in Britain, at 350 metres above sea level.

After British Rail had twice failed to close the line, in the 1960s and the 1980s, even the stations along its route have now been restored. Michael Portillo was instrumental in saving the line from certain closure in 1989 when, as transport minister, he convinced then Prime Minister Margaret Thatcher to refuse the second British Rail application to shut it down. He has since said that he considers the part he played in saving the railway line to be one of his greatest achievements in politics.

THE FORMER FUTURE BRITISH PRIME MINISTER

Michael Portillo was for many years a Conservative Party politician, a loyal supporter of Margaret Thatcher who went on to serve as a cabinet minister under John Major. He was once tipped to become leader of the party himself and, by extension, a future prime minister. With that kind of hardcore political stuff on your curriculum vitae, you probably don't aspire to be everyone's cup of tea, so it has come as something of a surprise that Michael Portillo, since retiring from politics, has gone on to become one of Britain's favourite TV and radio presenters.

His passion for rail travel was reinforced while serving as transport minister under Margaret Thatcher in the late 1980s, so perhaps it is less of a surprise that his many programmes in recent years have included the ever-popular *Great British Railway*

Journeys and *Great Continental Railway Journeys*. His unbounded enthusiasm for rail travel, his easy connection with people from all walks of life and his I'll-have-a-go-at-anything presenting style have won him many fans, and the journeys he describes are inspiring a new generation of travellers to take to the rails.

GLACIER EXPRESS (SWITZERLAND)

Something of a misnomer, really, as the train takes 8 hours to cover the 180 miles between Zermatt and St Moritz in the Swiss Alps, but you have to concede that it's probably a bit quicker than walking across 291 ravines and burrowing through 91 mountainsides to reach your ski resort. The track is narrow-gauge (including the longest narrow-gauge tunnel in the world), switching to rack-and-pinion when the going gets tough, and tunnel-and-pass-over-yourself spirals when the going gets even tougher. Creature comforts on board the Glacier Express include warmth, good food in lavish dining cars and glass roofs for your panoramic viewing pleasure. If snow and ice aren't your things, the summer views still live up to that Alpine jigsaw you put together as a kid.

JUNGFRAU RAILWAY (SWITZERLAND)

If you always wanted to climb the Eiger, one the most difficult and dangerous mountains in the world, but feel less keen about risking your life in the process, you could always scale the infamous north face by train.

The cogwheel, metre-gauge Jungfrau Railway in Switzerland runs from the picturesque mountain village of Kleine Scheidegg through tunnels that have been forged into the Eiger and Mönch mountains to arrive 50 minutes later at Jungfraujoch, Europe's highest railway station at 3,454 metres above sea level. There you can relax in a restaurant while taking in the breathtaking views of nearby glaciers and peaks. Step outside and the views will literally take your breath away because, until you have acclimatised to the altitude, it will feel as if somebody is trying to insert a sharp ice cube in your throat.

If you can't get to Switzerland, you can still see the train and its stunning locations by watching the 1975 film *The Eiger Sanction*, the assassination thriller starring and directed by Clint Eastwood.

ANY TRAIN TO THE SOUTH OF FRANCE

Whether you choose a superfast TGV or something a little slower, the best journey to take in France is from Paris down to the French Riviera. In a matter of hours you will enjoy a complete change of terrain, temperature and light: it is not uncommon on that journey to remove at least one layer of clothing and don your sunglasses. You can't 'sense' a journey like that travelling by plane, which is one of the reasons the French have managed to entice many domestic plane passengers back onto the tracks in recent years.

OSLO–BERGEN LINE (NORWAY)

If oxblood wooden cabins dotted around crystal-clear fjords float your (Viking) boat, and you like the idea of travelling across plateaux devoid of human activity, you will love the entire range of scenery along the Oslo–Bergen Line. Highlights along the 310-mile route between Norway's capital and its scenic second city (which takes around 6 hours 30 minutes to travel) include year-round snow views above the treeline and a station so remote that there are no roads to or from it. This is the territory in which Scott's team chose to train prior to their ill-fated expedition to the Antarctic in 1912, and which the makers of the 1980 Star Wars epic *The Empire Strikes Back* chose to represent the icy planet of the Hoth system.

The line is also popular for the opportunity to alight at Myrdal and take the spectacular branch line excursion down to Flåm. It is the steepest standard-gauge railway in Europe and comes with an astonishing view of the Sognefjord (Norway's longest and deepest fjord) below as the train twists slowly down the mountain.

ORIENT EXPRESS (EUROPE AND SOUTH EAST ASIA)

Step back in time and party like it's 1899, or the roaring twenties, or any other time that takes your fancy since the Compagnie Internationale des Wagon-Lits started to run its services from Paris in 1883. The current incarnation of the Orient Express continues to evoke an age when the style and romance of the journey were at least as important as the destination, and the art deco opulence of your carriage was up to the standard of the luxury hotel you were headed for. Sparkling crystal, polished wood and plush fabrics positively abound, and the dress code for dinner is sophisticated elegance. Dinner is always served on time, because long gone are the days when an irritating Belgian detective was allowed to hold up the next meal in order to have a denouement in the dining car, or when the train had to move to a siding to count the number of passengers who had not yet been murdered.

The European cities you can visit in such luxury today include Paris, Venice, Stockholm and Vienna. If you would prefer something a little sultrier, the Eastern and Oriental Express allows you to have a similar (but smart-casual) experience on the 1,200-mile Bangkok–Kuala Lumpur–Singapore line. Travelling in Japanese-built coaches that once plied their trade in New Zealand (on the Silver Star service), the views from the train will include many more rubber plantations and paddy fields than you are likely to see en route to Vienna.

GOLD-MEDAL SERVICE

Renowned as the founder of the Compagnie Internationale des Wagons-Lits, the railway company that ran the Orient Express service, Georges Nagelmackers took some time off to represent Belgium at the 1900 Olympic Games in Paris. He competed in the equestrian mail coach event, which involved racing mail coaches pulled by a four-horse team. As you would expect from the man who provided first-class service in everything he did, he took the gold medal.

MAHARAJAS' EXPRESS (RAJASTHAN, INDIA)

Of all India's magnificently named luxury trains (witness the *Royal Rajasthan on Wheels*, the *Golden Chariot*, the *Deccan Odyssey*, the *Palace on Wheels*), the *Maharajas' Express* is arguably the most luxurious and surely the most magnificently named. It is also one of the most expensive luxury trains on the planet. One of its tours, the Heritage of India, provides a week-long trip from Mumbai to New Delhi that takes in the lakes and palaces of Udaipur, the blue city of Jodhpur, the pink city of Jaipur, Ranthambore for a bit of tiger-spotting, and Agra for the Taj Mahal. When you are not being struck dumb by the destinations, you spend your time being struck dumb by the opulence of the train itself, especially if you can afford over $20,000 per person for the presidential suite, which takes up an entire carriage in order to accommodate the sitting-cum-dining room and the en suite master and guest bedrooms. If you're going to take the Maharaja's express, you might as well live like him while you're on board.

'TOY TRAIN' TO DARJEELING (INDIAN HIMALAYAS)

Staying within India, but at the other end of the financial scale from the *Maharajas' Express*, you can take the Darjeeling Himalayan Railway for a fistful of rupees. Completed in 1881, the line climbs 2,134 metres up into the Himalayas from Siliguri in West Bengal. It is one of the narrow-gauge mountain railways designed by the British to reach the relative cool of their hill stations in the summer (in this case, to escape the fierce heat of Calcutta).

It conquered 48 miles of mountainous terrain with frequent loops, spirals, zigzags and hideously sharp curves, and needed the narrowest of narrow gauges (0.6 metres) and the smallest of tank engines (B Class 0-4-0ST) to achieve the tortuous climb, although nowadays small diesel engines also take their turn. Surprisingly for a mountain railway, there are no tunnels, which means that you get to enjoy the scenery all the way up, including close-ups of hill towns and villages and, of course, the world-famous tea plantations. Clouds permitting, you may also be rewarded with a panoramic view that includes Mounts Everest and Kangchenjunga, two of the world's three highest mountains.

The journey today may continue to evoke the bygone era of the Raj, but it also remains a very Indian experience and it is all the better for it.

BLUE TRAIN AND ROVOS RAIL (SOUTH AFRICA)

If endless savannah, wild animals and stunning sunsets are more your thing, hop on board the *Blue Train* (not to be confused with the French Riviera version) for its sedate 27-hour, 994-mile journey across South Africa between Pretoria and Cape Town. Often heralded as the most lavish train in the world, its sapphire-blue carriages are at the luxury end of the scale. Services include 24/7 on-call personal butlers and strictly formal dining in plush surroundings, although the recommended dress code for lunch is scaled down to 'elegant casual'. If you haven't blown your entire savings on the trip itself, fear not, you can easily blow the rest in the on-board jewellery boutique.

If you want to make the journey at an even more sedate pace, but at the same standard of luxury, rival company Rovos Rail takes an extra day and night to cover the distance. Both companies claim to run the most luxurious train in the world, and they're probably both not far wrong.

TRANS-SIBERIAN RAILWAY (RUSSIA AND CHINA)

The main line of the Trans-Siberian Railway covers 6,152 miles to deliver passengers to stations between Moscow and Vladivostok on the Sea of Japan. It is Russia's main transport artery, carrying 30 per cent of the country's export freight and most of its domestic passenger traffic. If you want the ultimate first-class tourist experience, attended night and day by smiling, deferential staff, try the private Golden Eagle service. If you consider yourself more traveller than tourist, however, you might prefer that most Russian of experiences, the state-run Rossiya ('Russia') service, where smiling and deference can be harder to find. Either way, the journey takes 8 days and crosses seven time zones in conquering the icy wastes of southern Siberia. In terms of scenery, think *Dr Zhivago* and your expectations should be met.

There is also a Moscow–Beijing alternative on the Trans-Siberian Railway, serviced by a Chinese train, the Trans-Mongolian Express. It uses the same line as the Moscow–Vladivostok service until it drops down from Siberia to travel through Mongolia and the Gobi Desert on its way to the Chinese capital.

SHINKANSEN (JAPAN)

If it's an adrenalin rush you're after, or if you're just in a hurry to say you've been on one of the great railway journeys of the world, head straight to Japan. The bullet train is not so named for nothing, so don't be surprised if the experience feels more like a rocket launch than a train journey. There are many routes to choose from, including Tokyo to Kyoto. You'll feel as if you're on one of the faster rides at Disneyland, except you can't get off for 2 hours and 10 minutes, in which time you get to travel 325 miles. The other, and probably the best, reason for choosing this route is that you get to see the iconic view of Mount Fuji from the train, though you'd better be quick if you want to get a selfie on the way past.

GHAN AND INDIAN PACIFIC (AUSTRALIA)

Although the line that sought to cross the vast Australian continent from top to bottom was begun in 1878, it wasn't until 2004 that the top end from

Alice Springs to Darwin was finally completed. Until 1929 the last leg of the journey north had been an Afghan camel ride into Alice Springs, hence the name of the train service, the Ghan. The complete service takes 48 hours to cover the 1,852 miles of outback and more outback and even more outback from Adelaide to Darwin, with kangaroo-spotting the recommended way to while away the hours. If booking a package deal, the one optional excursion you might find difficult to resist is the overnight coach trip from Alice Springs to witness the glowing red sandstone of Uluru.

Of course, you can also cross Australia from side to side, this time on the Indian Pacific service, so called because the journey takes you all the way from Perth, on the Indian Ocean, to Sydney, on the Pacific. You will need an extra night to cross the continent this way, because the route, at 2,704 miles, is somewhat longer than the Ghan, and includes the longest dead-straight stretch of track in the world, running for 297 miles across the arid Nullarbor (from the Latin *nullus arbor*, meaning 'no tree') Plain.

ROCKY MOUNTAINEER (CANADA)

The most scenic Rocky Mountaineer trip is the 2-day tour that runs over the original Canadian Pacific track between Vancouver and Calgary. Even by Canadian standards the mountain scenery is hard to beat, and highlights, as you will know from every worldwide holiday brochure you have ever seen, include Banff and Lake Louise. The train cuts through the Rockies along the magnificently named Kicking Horse Canyon, one of the many places where you should keep your eyes open for bald eagles and grizzlies. Unlike many other luxury trains, this one only travels during daylight hours, with passengers overnighting instead in a Kamloops hotel and thereby being relieved of the irritation of squandering their savings on panoramic views of darkness.

CALIFORNIA ZEPHYR (USA)

This is the Amtrak service that seeks to relive the glory days of America's transcontinental trains, the railroad equivalent of Route 66, if you will. Running between Chicago, Illinois and Emeryville, California, which sits on San Francisco Bay, highlights include crossing the Rockies between Denver, Colorado and Salt Lake City, Utah, and traversing the Sierra Nevada between Reno, Nevada and Emeryville. Use the observation car whenever you can to maximise your viewing pleasure of the many mountains, canyons, rivers, lakes, prairies and big skies that are yours to behold for 51 hours 20 minutes across seven states and three time zones.

HIRAM BINGHAM (MACHU PICCHU, PERU)

The luxury train service that covers the journey from Cusco to the lost city of the Incas at Machu Picchu is named after Hiram Bingham, the American explorer who rediscovered the ruins in 1911. The blue-and-gold train is impressive, the views of Peruvian villages and llama herds are quite splendid, and the on-board Peruvian meals are a treat, but it is still difficult to argue that this rail service is all about the journey, not when the destination is at or near the top of most people's bucket lists. One surprising thing for many people about the rail journey, though, is that it is downhill. Although Machu Picchu is 2,350 metres above sea level, the starting point at Cusco is considerably higher, at 3,400 metres. Hence the train needs to descend into the Sacred Valley of the Andean foothills before following the Urubamba River to Aguas Calientes (Hot Springs), from where you need to climb by bus, or on foot, 1,280 feet back up again to Machu Picchu itself.

EINSTEIN'S TRAINS
OF THOUGHT

Everyone knows that Albert Einstein often used trains in his analogies to explain difficult stuff to simple people. For example, he might illustrate his theory of relativity by explaining that a slow train on the horizon was in fact travelling at the same speed as one rushing past you on a station platform, or that passengers seated in a moving train would see a baby crawling along their carriage at a speed of x, while someone looking in from the platform would see the same baby crawling along at a speed of $x + y$. He presumably left it to ordinary folk to figure out why unattended babies were allowed to crawl along moving trains in the first place.

ACROSS CITIES, MOUNTAINS AND SEAS

There is nothing like a train journey for reflections.

Tahir Shah

More often than not linked to the main railway lines, designed to transport passengers and freight from one town or city to another, the world's biggest cities depend on their own metropolitan networks to the extent that they would soon come to a shuddering halt without them. At the other end of the scale, many unique systems have branched away from main lines into more remote corners to meet the specific needs of the communities they serve. Metropolitan systems tend to run beneath, above or alongside clogged-up road networks, while community railways are more likely to have been built to link towns and villages across difficult terrain, or to generate much-needed income from the world's tourists. Let us first look beneath the surface.

UNDERGROUND RAILWAYS

As we have seen, London led the way in 1863 when it decided to go underground with a rail network that survives to this day. Budapest followed suit in 1896 and many others have been added around the world ever since, to the extent that there are now getting on for a couple of hundred underground systems in over fifty different countries. Here are some facts and figures about just a few of the underground systems that now exist (or mostly exist) below the surface of planet earth:

The **Seoul Metro** in South Korea is one of the cleanest, most efficient and most technically advanced passenger services in the world, having digital multimedia broadcasting, high-speed 4G, Wi-Fi and wireless broadband on every station and train. It is also the world's largest underground network, with 610 miles of track, and is therefore a rare combination of virtual and physical superhighway.

The **New York City Subway** in the USA has the most stations (468) and lines (24) of any underground system.

There are some fine examples remaining of the *fin-de-siècle* art nouveau style adopted at station entrances to the **Paris Métro** in France around the turn of the nineteenth century, including those to be found at Châtelet, Abesses and Porte Dauphine.

The shortest underground railway is the **Metropolitana di Catania** in Sicily. It runs for only 2.4 miles, and only half of that is underground.

The whole of Line 1 of the **Budapest Metro**, the first underground railway line to be built on the European mainland (in 1896), was designated a UNESCO World Heritage Site in 2002.

The longest single escalator on an underground station is at the Park Pobedy Station on the **Moscow Metro**. It is 127 metres long and takes 2 minutes 40 seconds to ride. As Moscow underground stations are widely regarded as the most beautiful in the world, this isn't really a problem.

The **Glasgow Subway** in Scotland is one of the world's shortest, with just 15 stations arranged in a circle. There are two tunnels, so that several trains can travel simultaneously in either a clockwise or anticlockwise direction. The livery of the trains became bright orange in 1980, and it wasn't long before Glaswegian humour had dubbed it the 'Clockwork Orange'.

The **Beijing Metro** in China carries the most passengers, with up to 11.5 million jumping on each day (it gets quite crowded).

MAIL RAIL

The London Tube is well known around the world, but not so many people know about the underground London Post Office Railway that came into service in 1927 to avoid the congestion of the world above. At its height, the railway carried over 20 million letters and packages a day at speeds of 30 mph below Oxford Street, extending for a total of 6.5 miles between Paddington to the west and beyond Liverpool Street to the east. It operated until 2003, when the growth of email finally put paid to the need for it.

RAILWAYS IN THE SKY

Some cities have preferred to look up to ease their congestion. This has been great news for tourists in particular, because these sky-high systems offer a low-cost bird's-eye view of some of the world's greatest cities while transporting us to and from airports, hotels, sporting venues and attractions. Just like underground systems, they also provide a wonderful insight into the daily life of these cities because we get to share the space with locals travelling to and from their workplaces, shops and schools. Here are just a few examples of the aerial pleasures available to us today:

Docklands Light Railway (London, England)

It is worth travelling on this driverless, elevated railway just to see the magnificently regenerated Docklands area. The visual treats for passengers include the River Thames, the O2 arena (Millennium Dome) and Canary Wharf.

Bangkok Skytrain (Thailand)

If ever a city needed an air-conditioned, sky-high transport system, it was Bangkok. Stay luxuriously cool while pitying the hot, seething mass of humanity below as it mixes with the exhaust fumes of gridlocked traffic. It is an exotic experience to travel with Bangkokians, while temple-spotting from the air passes the time nicely if you do get bored mingling with the locals.

Monorails (Various)

Once the preserve of the world's theme parks and then airports, elevated urban monorail systems have been springing up around the world in recent times, including those in Mumbai (India), Kuala Lumpur (Malaysia), Tokyo (Japan), Dubai (UAE) and Las Vegas (USA).

H-Bahn (Dortmund and Düsseldorf, Germany)

The Hängebahn (hanging railway) systems on Dortmund University campus and at Düsseldorf airport are driverless, suspended railways. If you think this sounds like a terribly modern idea, you're wrong (see below).

'WE ARE PLEASED TO ANNOUNCE THAT ALL SERVICES HAVE BEEN SUSPENDED UNTIL FURTHER NOTICE'

The Wuppertal Suspension Railway (*Wuppertaler Schwebebahn*) is one of the most unusual metropolitan systems in the world, having transported passengers in its hanging carriages above the German city of

Wuppertal since 1901. It takes 30 minutes to travel along underneath the monorail for the entire 8.3-mile journey.

In 1950, a circus decided to transport a baby elephant along the line as a publicity stunt, but the poor animal became frightened and crashed out of the carriage into the River Wupper 12 metres below. Miraculously, it sustained only minor injuries and the train operator and circus director got off with fines.

FUNICULAR RAILWAYS

Funicular railways tend to have two counterbalancing trains navigating a steep slope while attached to the same cable. In very simple terms, this means that the force of the down train helps to pull the other train up, following which the 'up train' repays the favour on the way back down. The first modern funicular railway designed to get citizens up and down a steep slope opened in Lyon, France in 1862. Budapest, on the Buda side going up to the castle, followed in

1890 (although it did have to be rebuilt after being bombed to bits during World War Two). The idea soon caught on and many of the world's steepest hills were soon being conquered by funicular, including the following worthy examples:

 The world's steepest passenger-carrying funicular railway is the **Katoomba Scenic Railway** in the Blue Mountains of New South Wales in Australia. The 52-degree (122 per cent) climb achieves a vertical lift of 206 metres and is perfect for acclimatising you for what comes next: hanging over the gorge below on the Katoomba Scenic Skyway cable car.

 The **Peak Tram** that carries passengers up to the higher reaches of Hong Kong Island had three classes when it opened for general service in 1890: first class was for British colonial figures and Victoria Peak residents; second class was for British military and Hong Kong police; and third class was for all other humans and animals. They all got the same view back down over Victoria Harbour, Lamma Island and the business district.

The English seaside resort of Bournemouth has three funiculars to carry passengers between the beach and the clifftop town, including the world's smallest, the **Fisherman's Walk Cliff Railway,** which is only 39 metres long.

 Montmartre Funicular in Paris has been taking grateful tourists up to the basilica of Sacré-Cœur and the artist colony at Place du Tertre since 1900. The alternative is 300 steps, but many people find them easier on the way down!

 There are around three hundred private mini-funiculars in the hilly city of **Wellington, New Zealand** to get residents and their shopping home.

 The **Cairn Gorm Funicular** in the Scottish Highlands is the longest (1.2 miles) and highest (1,097 metres) funicular railway in Britain. The panoramic view from the top is breathtaking and, on the day I was there, included a rainbow 200 metres below and a rare opportunity to see some mountain-dwelling ptarmigans.

There are three **Lisbon funiculars** to transport locals and tourists alike up and down the steep slopes of the Portuguese capital: the Lavra, the Gloria and the Bica. The Lavra was the world's first street funicular when it opened in 1884, and it continues to conquer the 25 per cent gradient of the Largo da Anunciada today. All three funiculars are amongst the world's most photogenic, resplendent in their iconic canary-yellow livery, and are definitely the world's most intimate: as they carry you up and down the narrow, winding streets, sometimes just inches from the doors and windows of the tall buildings they rub shoulders with, you can at times see inside houses and even smell family dinners being cooked.

FUNICULÌ, FUNICULÀ

Having failed to learn the lessons of AD 79, the Neapolitan authorities gave permission in the late nineteenth century for Thomas Cook (those well-known funicular-railway builders!) to build a funicular railway to the top of Mount Vesuvius. The famous Neapolitan song 'Funiculì, funiculà' (meaning 'funicular up, funicular down') was composed in 1880 to celebrate its opening.

Destroyed three times following eruptions in the twentieth century, they finally gave up on the railway following the last major eruption, in 1944, but talk of rebuilding the line has sprung up again in recent years. When questioned about the safety of such a proposal, a spokesman for the regional transport authority was quoted as saying, 'If it erupts, it erupts.' Having never been one to let molten lava put me off my next train journey, I'm definitely up for it.

MOUNTAIN RAILWAYS

We have already looked at some mountain railways in the Great Railway Journeys chapter, which is not surprising because mountain railways are by their very nature wonderfully scenic. They are also monuments to the men who built them, who somehow managed to triumph over nature in its most inhospitable form. More often than not, as we have seen, they were built with narrow-gauge track, which is more suited to the twists and turns necessary to negotiate mountainsides. A general rule of thumb is 'big mountain, small railway'. Here are some more climbing railways that will literally take your breath away when you get to the top, and leave you wondering whether there is anything that raw human endeavour cannot achieve when it puts its mind to it:

In 1865 the world's first steam-driven, narrow-gauge railway carried quarry slate and passengers between the quarry town of **Blaenau Ffestiniog**, 230 metres above sea level, and the harbour in Porthmadog below. This magnificent line in north Wales is operational today as a restored heritage railway.

———

The **Harz Mountain Railway Network** in northern Germany is a good, old-fashioned, proper railway system. Across a narrow-gauge network of 87 miles straddling the old border between east and west, its huge locomotives include 1950s 2-10-2T steam locomotives working their 14 wheels off to get up and over the mountain range day after day, year after year, in all weathers; the diesel locomotives are equally impressive. For tourists and rail enthusiasts, it is a wonderful step back in time to the golden age of steam, vintage diesel and sheer muscle power. For the citizens of the many mountain towns and villages connected by the network, it is their lifeline. It gets them to work and to the shops, and it gets their children to school.

The **Snaefell Mountain Railway** on the self-governing Isle of Man is the only surviving operational Fell railway system in the world. Fell railway systems, named after their English designer John Barraclough Fell and not because they climb fells (which they do), employed a raised third rail between the outer two rails for extra traction and braking, and were once used in France, Italy, Brazil and New Zealand. On a clear day, the views from the top of Snaefell, the highest point on the island, are said to stretch across six kingdoms: the Isle of Man, England, (Northern) Ireland, Scotland, Wales and Heaven.

The **Mountain Railways of India** have been designated a UNESCO World Heritage Site on account of the profound impact they had on social and economic development in the late nineteenth/early twentieth century, because they served as models for many others around the world, and because they remain living operational examples of engineering genius.

The three railways that comprise the 'site' are the Darjeeling Himalayan Railway in the north-east of the Himalayas, the Kalka–Shimla Railway in the north-west of the Himalayas, and the Nilgiri Mountain Railway in the southern state of Tamil Nadu. In other words, they are nowhere near each other, but all three offer stunning views of their respective terrains.

———————

One of the main problems with the Klondike Gold Rush of the 1890s was the need to get equipment-laden mules to and from the US port of Skagway (at the top of Alaska's Inside Passage) over the White Pass of the Coast Range Mountains. The **White Pass and Yukon Railroad** from Skagway to Whitehorse in Canada's Yukon Territory would ultimately provide the answer, but only after the gold rush had come and gone in 1900. As luck would have it, copper, silver and lead were found in greater abundance than gold and the railroad was in business. In recent years a large part of it has been restored to provide a mountain-railway excursion to the 800,000 cruise-ship passengers who turn up in Skagway each year.

THE TALE OF 'SOAPY' SMITH

As if it wasn't difficult enough to build the White Pass and Yukon Railroad over the high, rugged territory between Alaska and the Yukon Territory (450 tons of explosives and quite a few pick-axe-wielding navvies were needed), 'Soapy' Smith made it even harder. The Old West crime-gang boss tried everything to sabotage the railway, as it would prevent him from extorting tolls from mule-driving prospectors as they crossed over the mountain. A vigilante gang was set up to deal with the problem and 'Soapy' met his end in a shootout in 1898. The railroad resumed blasting after helping to capture the rest of the gang by blocking off their escape routes.

TRAIN FERRIES

Train ferries are so called because they have railway tracks that allow carriages on a through service to roll onto a boat at one harbour and roll back off again at a different harbour on the other side of the body of water in question. Their heyday may have come and gone, many such services having been replaced by increasingly sophisticated rail bridges and tunnels, but they are still more common than you might think:

➤ In 1850, the *Leviathan*, the world's first modern train ferry, started to operate on a roll-on/roll-off basis across the **River Tay** in Scotland. Known as the 'Floating Railway', it ran until replaced by the Tay Rail Bridge in 1890.

➤ Starting in 1936, British Rail used a night-time train ferry across the **English Channel** so that their passengers could get from London to Paris overnight without needing to leave their sleeping compartments. The last such night ferry ran in 1980, by which time cheaper airfares had rendered the business uncompetitive.

➤ The biggest roll-on/roll-off train ferry in the world is the MV *Skåne*, built in 1998 to carry freight trains (and trucks) across the **Baltic Sea** between Trelleborg in southern Sweden and Rostock in northern Germany. Its eight railway tracks, including two that are lowered to a deck once they are laden with railway carriages, cover a total distance of 0.68 miles. You can also cross the Baltic Sea as a passenger on the high-speed Hamburg-Copenhagen line, while your train has a well-earned rest between Germany and Denmark on the Puttgarden-Rødby ferry.

Other train ferries that continue to transport freight and/or passenger trains include those that cross the following waterways of the world:

➤ **Messina Strait:** carries passenger and freight trains between Calabria in the toe of Italy and Messina on Sicily.

➤ **Caspian Sea:** there are (mainly freight) train ferries across this stretch of water, linking the railways of Azerbaijan with those of Turkmenistan.

➤ **Gulf of Alaska and northern Pacific Ocean:** tugboats pull train-ferry barges between Alaska and the contiguous USA at Seattle. This is a long way to tug a train ferry but the alternative of building a railroad the length of the Coast Range Mountains (largely through Canada) doesn't bear thinking about.

➤ **Cook Strait:** the Interisland Express ferries freight trains back and forth between Wellington on the North Island and Picton on the South Island of New Zealand.

➤ **Qiongzhou Strait:** carrying freight and passenger trains between mainland China and Hainan Island. These are very choppy waters, so getting the boat tracks lined up horizontal with those on the harbour is no mean achievement.

FAST-FLOWING RUGBY

If you've ever thought how convenient Cardiff Central Station is for the city's two great rugby stadiums, Cardiff Arms Park and the Millennium Stadium, thank Isambard Kingdom Brunel. The River Taff once had a bit of a kink right where Brunel wanted to build the station, so he diverted it out of the way (nothing was allowed to obstruct the Great Western Railway). After the station opened in 1850, the Bute family who owned the reclaimed land between the station and the new path of the river decided to give it over to the people of Cardiff for recreation and sport. Voilà! (as they say in the Valleys).

WE'VE ALL DONE IT

If you told me you'd never left as much as a scarf or a pair of gloves, an umbrella or a mobile phone on a train, I probably wouldn't believe you. During my own commuter years, I left at least 6 million umbrellas on trains, usually when I'd had a few drinks and always when it was raining cats and dogs as I left the station. Here are some more unusual items that have actually been left on trains, none of them by me:

➤ Wooden prosthetic arm (probably just the result of a bit of armless fun)

➤ Giant inflatable Mickey Mouse (possibly left by somebody taking the mickey – or not)

- ➤ Silicone breast implant (bet she was glad to get that off her chest, though)

- ➤ Wedding dress (not sure if the train was still attached, but it would be quite ironic)

- ➤ Jar of bull's sperm (not entirely sure how the railway company knew that's what it was)

- ➤ Two human skulls (now that's what you call a delayed train!)

- ➤ Vasectomy kit (perhaps it had been left in a cutting)

- ➤ Kitchen sink (just in case you thought it was everything but!)

TRAINS ON FILM

There was no doubt in my mind that steam engines all had definite personalities.

Reverend W. Awdry

As all film buffs know, the first moving film ever seen by a cinema audience was of a train coming into the gare de La Ciotat in the south of France. The 50-second film was shot by the Lumière brothers in 1895 just after they had invented the movie camera. As the train drew closer to the screen, some members of the audience ducked down behind the seats in fear of their lives. Then, in 1903, the first movie ever to tell a story was the 12-minute-long *The Great Train Robbery*, a classic (silent) Western in which four bandits hold up a train with no violence spared.

Trains have continued to appear on screen ever since, in countless films and TV programmes around the world. They starred in many of the silent movies of the early twentieth century, a time in history when there seemed to be a constant need for heroes to untie damsels in distress from railway tracks seconds before they would have been cut in three by thundering steam locomotives (this led to the mistaken belief in Hollywood that 'standard gauge' on railroads was set at the average distance between the neck and ankles of a standard-issue damsel in distress).

Directors of the 'talkies' have also have found it difficult to resist the lure of train romances, hold-ups, hijacks and fights, especially fights that take place on the roof of a moving train as the inevitable tunnel looms ever larger at head height in the background. James Bond, Indiana Jones, the Lone Ranger, Zorro, Wolverine and Spider-Man are but a few of the action heroes who have had to survive 'Look-behind-you' moments while grappling with their arch enemies at rock and roll speed.

On television, there has been an explosion of railway-based programmes in recent years and the BBC in particular can't seem to get enough of them. The *Great British Railway Journeys* and *Great Continental Railway Journeys* programmes presented by Michael Portillo have already recreated hundreds of journeys that originally took place in Victorian Britain and dozens of Continental ones that took place in Europe just before the beginning of World War One.

There are too many train-related screenings to cover in anything less than the size of a small library, so here are just some of the best to allow you to relive some long-forgotten viewing pleasures, or perhaps prompt you to go and catch some others that you may have missed:

The General
(Buster Keaton, Clyde Bruckman, 1927)

One of the earliest (and best) full-length films to star trains on the big screen was *The General*, a silent movie full of dangerous train stunts and starring co-director Buster Keaton as Johnnie Gray, a Confederate railway engineer. Based on a real American Civil War incident, Union soldiers hijack a Confederate train (an American-type 4-4-0 locomotive), and Johnnie gives chase in another 4-4-0, the *Texas*, initially unaware that his true love, Annabelle Lee, is held captive on the stolen train ahead. In the best traditions of Hollywood, he eventually foils the pesky Yankees and recovers Annabelle. In the most expensive stunt of the silent-movie era, however, one of the locomotives does not have such a happy ending, being allowed to collapse into the river below as it crosses a sabotaged bridge in Cottage Grove, Oregon. After filming, the locomotive was left in its wrecked state in the riverbed as a minor tourist attraction for almost 20 years, until it was broken up for scrap in World War Two.

The 39 Steps
(Alfred Hitchcock, 1935)

Hitchcock was the first of three directors in the twentieth century to make a film based on John Buchan's 1915 novel. He cast Robert Donat as Richard Hannay, the man on the run (more often than not, by train) from eve-of-war Prussian spies, while Kenneth More (1959) and Robert Powell (1978) landed the plum role in the later versions. London St Pancras and Edinburgh Waverley are just two of the stations where Hannay has narrow escapes from his pursuers, and another hair-raising moment centres on his escape from the train on the iconic Forth Rail Bridge near Edinburgh (although the Victoria Bridge on the Severn Valley Railway stands in for the Forth Rail Bridge in the 1978 version, allowing Robert Powell to dangle from a much lower height than his two predecessors). Locomotives to star in the films included an A3 class Pacific (think *Flying Scotsman*) in 1935, and an A4 class Pacific (think *Mallard*) in 1959.

Hitchcock would return to the railways again and again for his film settings, most notably in *The Lady Vanishes* (1938), *Strangers on a Train* (1951) and *North by North-west* (1959).

Brief Encounter
(David Lean, 1945)

The classic film in which a married (but not to each other) middle-aged couple (played by Trevor Howard and Celia Johnson) fall in love following a chance meeting at Milford Junction, which was in fact Carnforth Station in Lancashire, then a junction of the London, Midland and Scottish Railway (one of the reasons Lean chose Carnforth as a filming location was that it was far enough away from the blackout zones that encircled the cities of wartime Britain at the time). The couple converge on the station from opposite directions on a weekly basis, and such is the film's enduring popularity that the waiting room where much of their doomed love affair unfolds has been restored in recent years to look as it did at the time of shooting. You can still travel by train to the Heritage Centre on the station and have a cup of tea, or even breakfast or lunch, in the *Brief Encounter* refreshment room: 'I'll have the Full English, but hold the doomed love affair.'

Like Hitchcock, train enthusiast Lean was also drawn time and again to the railways, not least for the setting of *The Bridge on the River Kwai* (1957) and for many of the scenes in *Doctor Zhivago* (1965).

The Railway Children
(Lionel Jeffries, 1970)

Based on Edith Nesbit's 1906 book of the same name, this classic children's film remains cult viewing for adults yearning for the age of innocence, steam and a cracking good yarn. Starring Dinah Sheridan, Bernard Cribbins and, as the children, Jenny Agutter, Sally Thomsett and Gary Warren, it centres on the desire of the Waterbury children to clear the name of their father, wrongly imprisoned as a spy. The children plan and plot in between waving to the trains that go by on the line near their home. As well as managing to clear their father's name with the help of an 'old gentleman' commuter and the local station porter (Bernard Cribbins), they also find time to avert a rail crash by warning an approaching train of a landslide (achieved through the waving of the girls' red petticoats), reunite a Russian dissident with his family and care for the old gentleman's grandson after he breaks a leg in a paper-chase accident.

There is no doubting the authenticity of the railway setting or the trains used in the film. It is set on the preserved Keighley and Worth Valley Railway in Yorkshire, including the station at Oakworth, and the steam locomotives used included a Lancashire and Yorkshire Railway Class 25 engine and a Nigel Gresley-designed Great Northern Railway Class N2 side-tank engine (which remains operational today on the Middleton Railway in West Yorkshire).

The same, alas, cannot be said for the authenticity of the children. Sally Thomsett was cast as 11-year old Phyllis but was in fact aged 20 at the time, while the 17-year-old Jenny Agutter played her 20-year-old big sister 'Bobbie'. Thomsett was not allowed to smoke, drink alcohol, see her boyfriend or drive her sports car anywhere near the set.

Murder on the Orient Express
(Sidney Lumet, 1974)

This is a British murder mystery based on the eponymous Agatha Christie novel, and the stars who wanted to spend time filming on board the Orient Express lined up thick and fast. They included Albert Finney (as Belgian sleuth Hercule Poirot), Richard Widmark, Lauren Bacall, Ingrid Bergman (who won an Oscar for her role), Sean Connery, John Gielgud, Vanessa Redgrave, Michael York, Jacqueline Bisset and Anthony Perkins. You get a better class of actor on the Orient Express.

The plot involves the need for Poirot to resolve the murder of an American ex-Mafia boss (Richard

Widmark) on board the Istanbul to London service. The victim is stabbed 12 times in the Balkans (and, let's be honest, there are few worse places to be stabbed in), while the train is stuck in a snowstorm. The absence of footsteps in the snow leads the cunning Poirot to deduce that the murderer or murderers remain on board. (Spoiler alert! In the film's denouement in the deluxe Pullman dining car, Poirot reveals that all 12 stabbers remained on board!)

Actual filming locations included the Gare de l'Est in Paris and, for running shots of the train and the snowbound murder scene, the Jura Mountains of the Alps. The steam locomotive used was a stalwart of the French railway system (SNCF) for 50 years, a 230 Class 4-6-0, known colloquially as the Ten Wheel (for a very obvious reason). This particular train, number 230 G 353, is said by SNCF to have starred in a total of 35 films, so it knew what was expected of it. There are rumours that it became something of a prima donna and that its 'rider' insisted on only Evian spring water being used in its tender.

Love on a Branch Line
(BBC TV mini-series, 1994)

This British television adaptation of John Hadfield's 1959 novel tells the delightful story of Jasper Pye, a refined civil servant sent to rural England to close down a less-than-useful statistical outpost run by three members of staff in the huge stately home that had been commandeered from Lord Flamborough during the Battle of Britain and subsequently forgotten about. Lord Flamborough, who lost both his legs in a train accident while working as an inexperienced driver during the 1929 General Strike, has long since taken up residence in a two-carriage train on a nearby private branch line. Jasper soon loses sight of his mission, falling instead for the idyllic countryside, as well as all three of Lord Flamborough's daughters.

Filming actually took place on the North Norfolk Railway, a heritage steam railway popularly known as the Poppy Line, and at Weybourne Station in particular, which had already starred as fictitious Walmington-on-Sea Station in the 1970s BBC sitcom *Dad's Army* and as equally fictitious Crimpton-on-Sea Station in the 1980s BBC sitcom *Hi-de-Hi!* The two carriages used by Lord Flamborough were third-class electric Pullman carriages that belonged to the Southern Railways 1930s art deco *Brighton Belle* service, many of whose carriages are currently being restored to their former glory for mainline use.

The Darjeeling Limited
(Wes Anderson, 2007)

This beautifully filmed madcap adventure about three brothers (played by Owen Wilson, Adrien Brody and Jason Schwartzman) travelling across India on a train is based on a misguided attempt by one of the brothers to get the three of them to bond with each other and at the same time achieve some spiritual enlightenment. The train sequences were filmed on the North Western Railway line that runs through the Thar Desert between the stunning Rajasthani cities of Jodhpur and Jaisalmer. Wes Anderson borrowed a diesel locomotive and ten carriages from the railway company and then revamped the carriages according to a design that was partially inspired by the interiors of the Twentieth Century Limited service that ran between New York and Chicago until 1967.

BOLLYWOOD ON RAILS

Bollywood is India's answer to Hollywood, but with more colour, action and dance routines. Its relationship with Indian Railways is a long and successful one, with countless love scenes and action sequences shot in, on and around trains, but one 7-minute sequence shot for the movie *Dil Se* (Mani Ratnam, 1998) stands out above the rest. It features Shah Rukh Khan (known to his millions of fans as SRK) and a cast of hundreds in a song and dance routine on top of a moving train as it snakes its way through the Nilgiri Mountain Railway in Tamil Nadu in the south of India. They gyrate to A. R. Rahman's chart-topping hit *Chaiyya, Chaiyya*, seemingly untroubled with the health and safety aspects of giving it your all on top of a moving train. It isn't just one of the great Bollywood moments; it is one of the great moments in cinematic history.

Harry Potter films
(various directors, 2001–11)

As all Harry Potter fans know, the *Hogwarts Express* leaves London King's Cross Platform 9¾ for Hogsmeade Station without fail at 11 a.m. on 1 September each year, and thereafter at the beginning of each term. Harry first meets Ron Weasley and Hermione Granger on the train and the trio go on to enjoy many a chocolate frog served by 'the witch with the tea trolley' during their long journeys together.

Towards the end of the journey the train is filmed passing along the real-life West Highland Line from Fort William to Mallaig (opposite the Isle of Skye), with the beautiful Glenfinnan Viaduct in particular featuring prominently in many of the shots. The *Hogwarts Castle* locomotive, originally built by the Muggles at Crewe to run on steam but now powered entirely by magic, is in fact the Great Western Railway Hall class 5972 *Olton Hall*, now based at the National Railway Museum at Shildon in County Durham. Your only chance as a Muggle to ride the *Hogwarts Express* is to hop on board the impressive replica that now runs between Universal Studios and Universal's Islands of Adventure in Florida.

Trans-Siberian
(Brad Anderson, 2008)

The legendary diesel-powered train journey from Beijing to Moscow provides the setting for this mix of murder, deception and drug-running. Woody Harrelson, Ben Kingsley and Emily Mortimer try their level best to outshine the iconic train and the Siberian scenery, but it's a tall order. An American couple, Roy (Woody Harrelson) and Jessie (Emily Mortimer), take the Trans-Siberian Express for the initial stage of their journey home from China, because Roy is a train enthusiast and can't resist the lure of the longest railway journey in the world. The excitement reaches levels even Roy could not have foreseen, though, when he has to take control of the locomotive himself in order to make good the couple's escape from villainous Russians. If only someone had told him that there was another train coming from the opposite direction along the same track…

The Taking of Pelham 1 2 3
(Tony Scott, 2009)

This is a remake of the 1974 film based on Morton Freedgood's book of the same name. The tense plot is centred on the armed hijacking of the 1.23 p.m. New York Subway train out of Pelham Bay Park, and a subsequent ransom demand in exchange for the lives of the passengers and train conductor who have been taken hostage. John Travolta plays the chief hostage-taker, while Denzel Washington had the critics drooling over his performance as the subway company employee on the other end of negotiations.

One of the main differences between the 1974 version (which starred Walter Matthau and Robert Shaw) and this one is that the earlier film was shot within Grand Central Station, whereas the 2009 version was filmed on carriages deep within the subway tunnels. This drive for claustrophobic authenticity came at a small price, though, as director Tony Scott, along with John Travolta, Denzel Washington and others working on the movie, had to take the NYC Transit Authority's 8-hour training course that is a prerequisite for anyone intending to walk on the rail tracks. Judge for yourself if the added authenticity was worth it. (It was.)

Downton Abbey
(ITV, 2010 onwards)

This classic British period drama is renowned as much for its attention to period detail as it is for its storylines and high quality of acting. It is not, therefore, surprising to learn that Downton Station is in fact the beautifully tended Horsted Keynes Station on the steam heritage Bluebell Railway in Sussex. If you want to travel in the post-Edwardian splendour enjoyed by Lord and Lady Grantham and the rest of the Crawley family, book a trip on the Bluebell Railway when they are running their first-class Pullman carriages. But do sit up straight!

Snowpiercer
(Bong Joon-ho, 2013)

Based on a French graphic novel of the same name, this South Korean sci-fi thriller with a star-studded Hollywood cast brings train films bang up to date. It is set in the future after a failed climate-change experiment kills everyone on the planet except those on board the *Snowpiercer*, a massive train that hurtles non-stop around the globe behind a perpetual-motion engine, over and over again. A class system and a divided economy are quickly established, and life on board the train becomes a microcosm of how the world was before disaster struck – until, 17 years on, the lower classes at the back of the train decide that enough is enough. The revolution (pun intended) is underway.

TRAINS IN THE ARTS

I never travel without my diary.
One should always have something
sensational to read in the train.

Oscar Wilde

Trains made a huge and immediate impact on the world when they burst into public consciousness, so it is not surprising that artists, lyricists, musicians, writers and poets soon sought to capture the essence and romance of rail travel in their works. In this chapter we will look at some of their most significant offerings.

AN ARTIST'S IMPRESSION

Trains were an exciting new subject for artists in the nineteenth century, presenting them with opportunities to depict the raw power of steam, capture motion within landscape and portray human reactions to the possibilities of travel. They certainly made an impression on the French Impressionists, many of whom took lodgings or a studio close to the Gare Saint-Lazare in Paris. Claude Monet was so fascinated by the golden age of steam trains that he painted the subject 11 times. In 1998 the Musée d'Orsay in Paris and the National Art Gallery in Washington, D.C. even put on an exhibition entitled *Manet, Monet and the Gare Saint-Lazare* – a particularly appropriate subject for the Musée d'Orsay, having itself been a railway station in a previous life.

But it wasn't just the Impressionists who were impressed. Here are some of the best-known masterpieces to grace our gallery walls:

Rain, Steam and Speed – The Great Western Railway

Artist: J. M. W. Turner
Year: 1844
Whereabouts: National Gallery, London
Description: A typically atmospheric depiction by the English Romantic landscape painter of a Gooch Great Western 4-2-2 steam locomotive racing across the Maidenhead Railway Bridge between London Paddington and Reading just six years after the line had opened. The intensity of light and colour soon had Monet and others studying Turner's technique.

The Travelling Companions

Artist: Augustus Egg
Year: 1862
Whereabouts: Birmingham Museum and Art Gallery, West Midlands
Description: Egg uses a train compartment as a Hogarth-style setting to depict the differences between two almost identically dressed Victorian ladies sitting opposite one another. One is perfectly prim and proper, industriously reading her book with her gloves on, a

basket of flowers at her side; the other displays signs of not adhering entirely to the Victorian values of the day, having given in to idleness by falling asleep, her hands gloveless and thereby exposed for all the world to see, and with a basket of (forbidden) fruit at her side. The train is travelling alongside the Mediterranean in the south of France, an area to which many Victorians, including Egg, travelled by train in the hope of improving their health.

Artist: William Powell Frith
Year: 1862
Whereabouts: Lady Lever Art Gallery, Liverpool, Merseyside
Description: A huge canvas by the English social painter of over a hundred characters at Paddington Station in London. The cast-iron and glass structure of the station and the steam locomotive would have appeared ultramodern at the time, and Frith makes a point of displaying the vast amounts of luggage that Victorians travelled with when they took to the rails.

THE MAN'S NOT EVEN DEAD!

When William Powell Frith's huge canvas of a London Paddington Station scene was first unveiled in 1862, *The Times* reported that he had been paid the staggering sum of £8,750 for it, going on to point out that such amounts had traditionally been reserved for the works of dead painters.

Lordship Lane Station, Dulwich

Artist: Camille Pissarro
Year: 1871
Whereabouts: Courtauld Institute of Art, London
Description: A small, soot-blackened steam locomotive, viewed from a footbridge, takes centre stage as it puffs towards us out of what was still then a rural station on the Crystal Palace and South London Junction Railway. What the Danish-French Impressionist painter depicted was the modernity of

a changing world, as suburban housing mushroomed at the same pace as an ever-growing rail network.

Artist: Édouard Manet
Year: 1873
Whereabouts: National Gallery of Art, Washington, D.C.
Description: French Impressionist Manet was one of those who took rooms near the Gare Saint-Lazare, the biggest and busiest station in Paris at the time. In fact, the doors to his studio are visible across the other side of that very railway station in this painting. A young girl clings to the railings as she gazes down at a steam locomotive on the tracks below, while the woman beside her sits with her back to the railings, perhaps having seen it all before.

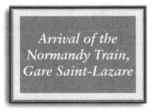

Artist: Claude Monet
Year: 1877
Whereabouts: Art Institute of Chicago, Illinois
Description: Fellow French Impressionist Monet takes us right inside the Gare Saint-Lazare, but still manages to convey the impression of a landscape

scene, with smoke from the trains taking on the role of clouds. He had to work quickly to capture the moment of light, steam and motion as trains arrived at the station, and the canvas now in Chicago is just one of seven that he painted of the station within three months to exhibit at the third Impressionist exhibition in Paris.

Le Train Bleu (The Blue Train)

Artist: Vincent van Gogh
Year: 1888
Whereabouts: Musée Rodin, Paris
Description: One of his four paintings that included a train, this is the view that the troubled post-Impressionist Dutch artist captured of a long, blue freight train as it crossed over the viaduct near Arles, as seen through the trees in a park. Arles is the town in the south of France where he stayed in 1888 in the 'yellow house', his painting of which that year also included a steam train in the background.

House by the Railroad

Artist: Edward Hopper
Year: 1925
Whereabouts: Museum of Modern Art, New York City
Description: Given his propensity for straight, clean lines, Hopper was always going to be able to make good use of railroad tracks, streamlined locomotives and railroad carriages. And he did, again and again. This particular painting, the very first to be acquired by the Museum of Modern Art in 1930, captured the isolation and loneliness of a railroad track in the middle of nowhere in between trains, with only an abandoned American Gothic mansion for company. It portrays the clash between the faded grandeur of a bygone rural way of life and the exciting world of modernisation brought about by the American railroad system – a struggle which, it seemed, could only have one winner.

Night Freight (Condor)

Artist: Terence Cuneo
Year: 1960
Whereabouts: Private collection
Description: English artist Terence Cuneo was an accomplished painter of many subjects and possibly most famous for being the official artist at the coronation of Queen Elizabeth II. He is known in railway circles for his depictions of trains, many of which have appeared on countless book jackets, catalogues, jigsaws, railway advertising posters and postage stamps. His originals can be seen in many British museums, galleries and other institutions, and a bronze statue of him by renowned Scottish sculptor Philip Jackson stands at London Waterloo Station as a memorial to his contribution to railway art.

The painting I have chosen here is the one he did of the 'Condor' night freight service that ran between London and Glasgow in the 1950s and 1960s, because I think it captures perfectly the immense power of a British Rail Class 28 diesel locomotive in full flow. The Class 28 was never in fact the most reliable of locomotives but you wouldn't think so to look at Cuneo's depiction of it.

THE POSTER ART OF NORMAN WILKINSON

English artist Norman Wilkinson was first and foremost a marine painter, who also put his skills to patriotic use when he designed the 'dazzle camouflage' that protected merchant ships during World War One. One of his marine paintings (*Plymouth Harbour*) hung in the first-class smoking room of the Titanic but is probably not in the best of condition by now.

He is also known to millions for the advertising posters that he designed and drew for the London and North Western Railway and the London Midland and Scottish Railway in the early twentieth century, enticing British and foreign tourists alike to come and sample the delights of the British Isles by train. There was nowhere that he didn't make look positively idyllic and he must have been responsible for countless numbers of rail holidays taken. In his posters, Colwyn Bay became the 'Gateway to the Welsh Rockies'; Belfast Lough was the 'Gateway to Happy Holidays'; Devon was the area to go to 'For Sunshine and Sea Breezes'; and the Scottish Highlands and Islands promised 'Holidays on Land and Sea'.

RAILWAY BATHING BEAUTIES

A London, Midlands and Scottish Railway poster produced in 1937 by Italian artist Fortunino Matania highlighted the charms of Southport Lido in Merseyside by displaying a slightly risqué (for its time) sketch of female bathing beauties. A copy of the poster was sold at auction in 2006 for £10,000, having been bought two weeks earlier for £14. That must have caused a titter or two at the back of the room.

MUSICAL TRAINS

Trains are by their very nature rhythmic so perhaps it was inevitable that they would find their way into every conceivable form of music, from classical to jazz and boogie-woogie, from blues and country to rock and pop. Here are some examples to illustrate the widespread appeal of the sound and romance of trains:

Tune: 'Pacific 231'
Style: Orchestral
Year: 1923
Recorded by: Arthur Honegger

The *mouvement symphonique* that propelled Swiss composer and train enthusiast Honegger to fame depicts the sound of a Pacific 231 steam locomotive, a class of locomotive that is more commonly known as a 4-6-2 (in many European countries the conventional notation counts axles rather than wheels, hence 2-3-1). The piece was later used as the soundtrack to a short film of the same name in 1949, a film that so vividly captured the majesty of the steam locomotive that it won the Short Film Palme d'Or at Cannes that year.

Tune: 'Chattanooga Choo Choo'
Style: Big-band swing
Year: 1941
Recorded by: Glen Miller and his Orchestra

After featuring in the 1941 musical film *Sun Valley Serenade*, this Oscar-nominated record was the first ever to receive a gold disc (1.2 million sold) and remained at number one for 9 weeks. It was written while the composers Harry Warren (music) and Mack Gordon (words) were travelling on the Southern

Railway's 'Birmingham Special' between New York City and Birmingham, Alabama via Chattanooga, Tennessee. The train they had in mind was not the one they were travelling on, though, as their inspiration apparently came from a 2-6-0 Mogul wood-burning steam locomotive on that same railroad.

The iconic song has since been covered by anybody who's anybody in the music business, including Cab Calloway, Carmen Miranda, Bill Haley & His Comets, Elvis Presley, The Shadows and Barry Manilow.

Tune: 'The Loco-Motion'
Style: Pop
Year: 1962
Recorded by: Little Eva

The song that everybody liked to line-dance to while pretending to be a train was written by Carole King and Gerry Goffin for Eva Boyd, the bubbly teenager who used to babysit for them. As Little Eva, the babysitter took the song to number one in the USA and number two in Britain. The appropriately named Grand Funk Railroad, an American blues rock band, took it back to the top of the US charts with an alternative version in 1974, and Australian pocket rocket Kylie Minogue had worldwide success in

1988 when she gave the song the Little Eva treatment all over again.

Tune: 'Last Train to Clarksville'
Year: 1967
Style: Pop/rock
Recorded by: The Monkees

The catchy debut single of the fun-loving quartet, who were soon to become America's answer to the Beatles. In the year that followed, in fact, they outsold The Beatles and The Rolling Stones put together. The lyrics constitute a plea from a young man about to be drafted into the Vietnam War that his sweetheart should hop on the last train to Clarksville, which was close to the US Air Force base in Tennessee from which many troops were sent overseas, so that they might spend some final moments together before he goes off to war.

Tune: 'Hear My Train A Comin'
Style: Blues rock
Year: 1967
Recorded by: Jimi Hendrix

Said to have been written by Hendrix to evoke the longing for the arrival of the all-important train that would take cotton pickers north to a better life after the American Civil War. He often performed the song live and it was also considered important enough to be one of the 12 tracks included in the 1973 'rockumentary' about the singer's life.

Tune: 'Casey Jones'
Style: Rock
Year: 1970
Recorded by: Grateful Dead

An update by the eclectic US band of the traditional folk song 'The Ballad of Casey Jones' on their 1970 *Workingman's Dead* album. The original ballad, most famously covered by American country legend Johnny Cash, and the Grateful Dead version, both referred to the true story of engine driver Casey Jones, who died in 1900 while trying to stop his collision-bound 4-6-0 'Ten Wheeler', the *Cannonball Express*. He slowed the train enough to save the lives of all passengers on board, but not his own, and a railroad legend was born. He later became immortalised not just in music, but also on film and in TV programmes bearing his name.

Tune: 'Midnight Train to Georgia'
Style: Soul
Year: 1973
Recorded by: Gladys Knight and the Pips

The song that even people who can't sing like to sing, this soulful classic became the band's Grammy-winning signature tune. If you'd rather live with him in his world than without him in yours, you should know by now when the next train leaves for his world.

Tune: 'Slow Train Coming'
Style: Gospel rock
Year: 1979
Recorded by: Bob Dylan

The title song of the album that Dylan wrote to declare himself a born-again Christian, it nonetheless sounded as Dylan as Dylan ever was and it benefited from having Mark Knopfler of Dire Straits fame on lead guitar. Whether it was meant to or not, the pen-and-ink album cover pays homage to the navvies who built the American railroad.

Tune: 'Crazy Train'
Style: Heavy metal
Year: 1980
Recorded by: Ozzy Osbourne

The very first single from the English legend's very first solo album (*Blizzard of Ozz*) begins with the words 'All aboard!' and has as its chorus, 'I'm going off the rails on a crazy train.' The guitar solo on the track is often voted one of the best of all time, Randy Rhoads, Ozzy's lead guitarist, clearly having been inspired by the rhythm of the train in his mind while he composed it.

Tune: 'Train Medley'
Style: Country hobo
Year: 1980
Recorded by: Boxcar Willie

One of many train compositions performed by the appropriately named country music singer, who sang in 'old-time hobo' style. Given that his albums included *Daddy Was a Railroad Man* and *King of the Freight Train*, and that he listed his instruments as 'guitar' and 'train whistle', most people knew of his passion for US railroads and trains. Not so many people knew that he was a US fighter pilot during the Korean War.

Tune: *Musique à grande vitesse* (High-speed music)
Style: Classical (for orchestra and ballet)
Year: 1993
Recorded by: Michael Nyman Band
and the National Orchestra of Lille

Written by English composer Nyman to commemorate the opening of the new Paris–Lille TGV (*train à grande vitesse*) line in 1993. When you listen to this piece, you won't be able to imagine yourself anywhere other than on a high-speed train racing through the French countryside. The ballet version is referred to as *Danse à grande vitesse* (High-speed dance).

Tune: 'Slow Train'
Style: Blues rock
Year: 2011
Recorded by: Joe Bonamassa

The prolific US singer/songwriter/guitarist is one of many artists who have helped to bring the train song bang up to date in the twenty-first century with this offering from his 2011 *Dustbowl* album, so don't expect trains to disappear from song lyrics any time soon.

TAKING TRAINS LITERALLY

Writers and poets have been just as keen as artists and musicians to jump on board the train wagon. Many writers, such as Agatha Christie, used trains as the setting for some of their most famous stories (*Murder on the Orient Express*; *The Mystery of the Blue Train*). Others, like Leo Tolstoy and Boris Pasternak, used them as thematic imagery throughout their epic tales (*Anna Karenina*; *Dr Zhivago*). P. G. Wodehouse even used them for comic effect, when he had Roderick Spode, the 'amateur dictator' of the Jeeves and Wooster books, announce the widening of the gauge of the entire British railway network 'so that sheep might stand sideways on trains'.

Authors of children's books have also made impressive use of trains to get their messages across, including, of course, the Reverend W. Awdry, whose best-selling stories from The Railway Series have made worldwide icons of Thomas the Tank Engine and his friends. Another children's author to personify trains to great effect was Arnold Munk, whose 1920 story of *The Little Engine That Could* inspired generations of children to give of their best in the knowledge that they could succeed if they only tried hard enough.

Here are just a few examples of the many train-related books and poems that have educated, entertained and inspired generations of readers and will continue to do so for many years to come:

Train stories

Title: *The Signalman*
Author: Charles Dickens
Year: 1866

A short story by the great English novelist centres around the eponymous signalman's visions of a ghost waving and shouting at him from the mouth of a nearby railway tunnel, and the fact that a rail tragedy of some kind or other inevitably occurs following each vision. Dickens wrote the story shortly after narrowly surviving a fatal rail accident himself. He had been on board when the London to Folkestone boat train derailed over a viaduct in June 1865, killing ten and injuring 40 passengers.

Title: *Through the Looking-Glass*
Author: Lewis Carroll
Year: 1871

In the sequel to *Alice's Adventures in Wonderland*, the English author puts Alice in a crowded railway carriage without a ticket. The guard inspects her through a telescope, a microscope and a pair of opera glasses before deciding that she is travelling in the wrong direction and leaving. The other passengers, including a goat, a beetle and a horse, make rude comments about her stupidity, but she soon forgets about all this when the train suddenly flies through the air to cross a brook and deposits Alice under a tree, next to a gnat. You just couldn't make it up!

Title: *Anna Karenina*
Author: Leo Tolstoy
Year: 1877

Near the beginning of *Anna Karenina*, a railway worker accidentally slips under a train in Anna's presence, which she considers to be a very bad omen. She's not wrong. The omen continues to haunt her as she is torn apart by her ill-fated love affair and doomed marriage. Trains appear throughout the novel in line with some of the more dramatic twists and turns of the plot, and at the end a desperate Anna commits suicide by throwing herself under a passing train, turning the earlier omen into a self-fulfilling prophecy.

Ironically, Tolstoy himself died in a Russian railway station (Astapovo) in 1910 after taking a train to escape his own troubled marriage. He contracted pneumonia on the train and the stationmaster offered him his bed on which to recuperate – a bed that would become his deathbed. He didn't get to die in peace over the course of the week he spent at the station, because the world's press had been able to get there quickly and easily on a kind of macabre railway special straight to the spot. In one of the earliest-known examples of frenzied media intrusion, newspaper reporters wired daily updates about nothing much to their various home countries, and were joined by a Pathé News camera team eager to catch any final glimpses to be had of the great man. They were, of course, all rewarded with a scoop when he did indeed pass away at the station.

Title: *La Bête Humaine*
Author: Emile Zola
Year: 1890

This psychological thriller by the French novelist was set on the Paris–Le Havre railway line and involved a train driver and a deputy stationmaster and his wife in murder, lust and infidelity. A train derailment, a rail suicide and a runaway train at the outbreak of the Franco–Prussian War all help to keep the action hurtling along the tracks, and evocative descriptions of engine drivers battling to control their steaming locomotive beasts add coal-bucketloads of atmosphere.

Title: *The Lost Special*
Author: Sir Arthur Conan Doyle
Year: 1898

A short story in which the Scottish writer has an unnamed 'amateur reasoner of some celebrity' investigate the disappearance of a privately hired train between Liverpool and London. The only people on board were the engineer, fireman, guard and two South Americans, but it turns out that the Italian Mafia are behind the disappearance.

In the 60 stories in which Conan Doyle put a name (Sherlock Holmes) to his 'amateur reasoner', 44 also involved rail travel. This is not too surprising, given that in Victorian Britain the only travel alternative was a horse-drawn coach: one simply cannot solve complex mysteries quickly while bouncing up and down rutted tracks on very little suspension, however elementary the solution might turn out to be.

GEORGE BRADSHAW IN LITERATURE

His fame may have been resurrected in recent years by the BBC series *Great British Railway Journeys* and *Great Continental Railway Journeys*, presented by former British cabinet minister Michael Portillo, but George Bradshaw was even more famous during the period his railway timetables and associated travel guides were actually in print (between 1839 and 1961).

His guidebooks were referred to countless times in popular literature, including Jules Verne's *Around the World in Eighty Days*, as Phileas Fogg sets off with his Bradshaw to conquer the world's circumference, and Bram Stoker's *Dracula*, in which the eponymous count refers to a Bradshaw's guide in planning how to get himself and his coffin from Whitby to London. Other popular writers to refer to a Bradshaw's guide include Charles Dickens, Sir Arthur Conan Doyle (there was always a copy of Bradshaw's at 221b Baker Street), Agatha Christie and Lewis Carroll, but perhaps Bradshaw's crowning literary glory remains the fact that a copy of his own 1863 railway guide was included in a time capsule under Cleopatra's Needle on London's Victoria Embankment in 1878, along with a set of British coins, a portrait of Queen Victoria, the Bible, and photographs of 12 of the best-looking English ladies of the day!

Title: *The Mystery of the Blue Train*
Author: Agatha Christie
Year: 1928

Hercule Poirot, the fictional Belgian detective created by the English novelist, is intent on minding his own business (but we all know better, don't we, boys and girls?) when he boards *Le Train Bleu* in Paris, bound for the French Riviera. One strangled American heiress, one missing ruby and one murderous male impersonator later, Poirot does what Poirot does best: solving complicated murders while minding his own business.

Title: The Railway Series
Author: Reverend W. Awdry and
Christopher Awdry
Year: 1945–2011

A total of 42 books have been written in the series, initially by the English cleric and rail enthusiast himself, and later by his son Christopher. At first glance, they are brilliantly simple children's stories about personified trains on the fictional Island of Sodor. On closer inspection, they are based on actual British railway lines and locomotives, and on real-life events such as the closure of branch lines throughout the UK in the 1960s and the replacement of steam by diesel. Illustrators have come and gone, as have narrators of the spin-off television series, but the popularity of the stories and characters is undiminished to this day.

It is also the case that many famous locomotives have made 'guest appearances' in The Railway Series. In book number 35, *Thomas and the Great Railway Show*, for example, Thomas gets invited to visit the National Railway Museum in York, where he can barely conceal his excitement at meeting *Rocket*, *Iron Duke*, *Mallard*, *Duchess of Hamilton* and *Green Arrow*.

The real-life Thomas and friends

If you have ever wondered which 'real-life' trains the Reverend W. Awdry chose as his models for The Railway Series, here are just a few to get you started:

FICTIONAL CHARACTER	ACTUAL LOCOMOTIVE	SERVICE HISTORY
Thomas the Tank Engine	Billinton 0-6-0T (tank) E2 Class steam locomotive	Shunting and short-haul freight services on the London, Brighton and South Coast Railway
Gordon the Big Engine	Gresley Pacific 4-6-2 A3 Class steam tender engine	Mainline passenger services on the London and North Eastern Railway
Henry the Green Engine	Stanier Class 5 4-6-0 steam tender engine	Utility locomotive on the London, Midland and Scottish Railway, known as the 'Black Five'

James the Red Engine	Class 28 0-6-0 steam tender engine	Passenger and freight services on the Lancashire and Yorkshire Railway
Bill and Ben	W. G. Bagnall 0-4-0ST (saddle tank) steam locomotives *Alfred* and *Judy*	Purpose-built for industrial service around tight curves and under low bridges in and around Par Harbour in Cornwall
Daisy	Class 101 DMU (diesel multiple unit)	The lightweight DMU that started to replace steam locomotives on UK branch lines in the 1960s
Pip and Emma	British Rail Class 43 InterCity 125 high-speed diesel	The high-speed train that still holds the world speed record for diesel trains

Title: *Strangers on a Train*
Author: Patricia Highsmith
Year: 1950

This was the American author's first novel, a psychological thriller in which two strangers meet on a train and discuss the possibility of swapping murders so that neither will have a motive in the eyes of the police. Charles Anthony Bruno, a psychopathic playboy, wants his father murdered, whereas Guy Haines, an architect, would quite like his wife out of the way so that he can take up with his mistress. Haines doesn't take Bruno's suggestion to swap murders too seriously, but he changes his tune after Bruno has murdered his wife. Haines eventually returns the favour but he lacks the nerve to live with his guilt and ultimately confesses all after Bruno has accidentally drowned.

Master of suspense Alfred Hitchcock turned the book into a film the year after its publication.

Title: *From Russia, With Love*
Author: Ian Fleming
Year: 1957

English novelist Fleming often had British secret agent 007 involved in train chases and train-top scraps, but in this novel he had his spy playing out much of the action on board the Orient Express. Copious amounts of intrigue, passion, personal combat, shootings and murder keep up the pace in the dining car and in the suite that Bond has booked for himself and the defecting Soviet beauty Tatiana Romanova. Bond makes a rare mistake when he is fooled into thinking that his would-be nemesis, a Russian executioner whose homicidal tendencies coincide with the full moon, is a fellow MI6 agent. That error occurs in the Pullman dining car when Bond glosses over the Russian's giveaway culinary faux pas when the latter orders red wine to go with his fish.

Title: Jim Stringer novels
Author: Andrew Martin
Year: since 2002

A series of detective novels by the contemporary English writer has railwayman Jim Stringer assigned to the London and Southwest Railway police in Edwardian England, where he solves a number of crimes before spreading his wings to do the same thing in further-flung places, including Iraq and India. You know that you are in for train-related literary treats just by looking at the book titles, which include *Necropolis Railway*, *Murder at Deviation Junction*,

Death on a Branch Line, *The Baghdad Railway Club* and *Night Train to Jamalpur*.

Train poems

Given that poetry and trains have rhythm in common, this was another inevitable union. In fact, such was the allure of the steam age in Britain that *Night Mail*, a 1936 documentary about the overnight London to Glasgow Postal Special train included a poem written specially by no less a poet than W. H. Auden and set to music by no less a composer than Benjamin Britten. The poem is recited to the rhythmic beat of the *Scots Guardsman* steam locomotive thundering down towards the Scottish border as the mail is being sorted in the carriages behind. Here are some other examples of riveting railway-related rhymes you might come across in the many poetry anthologies that exist to evoke the spirit of the railway:

Poem: 'From a Railway Carriage'
Author: Robert Louis Stevenson
Year: 1885

The Scottish novelist and poet included this poem in his collection *A Child's Garden of Verses*, in which he describes trains as 'faster than fairies' and 'faster than witches'. Stevenson was also a travel writer and by the age of 28 had crossed the USA by train from New York to California (although his primary reason for doing so was to resume a love affair with an older American woman).

Poem: 'On the Departure Platform'
Author: Thomas Hardy
Year: c.1910

The sweet sorrow of parting is perfectly encapsulated following a farewell kiss at a station ticket barrier, becoming increasingly poignant as the man left behind can only stand back and watch his sweetheart getting smaller and smaller as she walks down the 'diminishing platform'.

Poem: 'Adlestrop'
Author: Edward Thomas
Year: 1917

A wonderful description of a moment in time, captured when the poet was on a train that made an unscheduled stop on a hot summer's day in 1914 at the tiny village of Adlestrop in Gloucestershire. 'No one left and no one came' on account of the express train having stopped there 'unwontedly'.

Poem: 'Harrow-on-the-Hill'
Author: John Betjeman
Year: 1954

The English Poet Laureate was a great rail enthusiast who used the images and sounds of trains and railways and stations in a number of his poems. This one appeared in a collection called *A Few Late Chrysanthemums* and refers to the electric trains that are lit up 'after tea' in the melancholy of autumn. As we have seen, Betjeman was the saviour of St Pancras Station in the 1960s, and in 1973 he presented a TV documentary called *Metro-Land* about the growth of the Metropolitan Railway across north-west London in the early twentieth century.

Poem: 'The Whitsun Weddings'
Author: Philip Larkin
Year: 1964

The train poem to end all train poems, the English master of verse captures perfectly the many weddings he witnesses from his train seat as he travels one sunny Saturday afternoon from Kingston-upon-Hull (where he worked as a librarian) to London. He doesn't just spot weddings, though, he spots 'short-shadowed cattle', 'acres of dismantled cars', an Odeon cinema that 'went past', a cricketer running up to bowl. Travelling in the days when train windows could be opened properly, he is also able to capture the smells of early summer in the countryside and towns that he passes through.

THEATRICAL TRAINS

You might think that trains are not a natural fit for the theatre, but some playwrights and theatre impresarios beg to differ:

Play/Musical: *The Ghost Train*
Year: 1923–24

Written by Arnold Ridley, the English actor and playwright who went on to play Private Godfrey in the British sitcom *Dad's Army*, this play was a mystery thriller involving train passengers who had become stranded overnight at a disused railway station and then advised not to clap eyes on the ghost train that would pass through for fear of the inevitable death that would follow. The very next year saw the first production of *The Wrecker*, another of his plays with a train theme, this time concerning an old engine driver whose locomotive had become a bit too self-important. The production of both plays involved train appearances that required elaborate special effects for their day.

Play/Musical: *Starlight Express*
Year: 1984 onwards

It is said that the English musical impresario Andrew Lloyd Webber originally wanted to base a musical on Thomas the Tank Engine and his friends in The Railway Series books but that the Reverend W. Awdry wasn't prepared to give him the amount of poetic licence he wanted. Instead, his rock musical *Starlight Express* is based on toy trains racing around inside the dreams of a small boy, with the trains portrayed on stage by roller-skating actors. Steam, diesel and electric locomotives try to outdo one another to win the all-important race, with *Rusty*, the ageing steam locomotive, prevailing against all the odds. The Starlight Express did in fact exist as a service on British railways in the late 1950s and early 1960s, running during the night at weekends between London and Glasgow.

Starlight Express was one of the longest-running musicals in London's West End, from 1984 until 2002, and has toured worldwide. After 26 years, it remains one of the biggest shows in Germany.

Play/Musical: *The Railway Children*
Year: 2005 onwards

This is the theatre production of the 1906 Edith Nesbit book that also enjoyed great success as a film of the same name in 1970. Since first being adapted for the stage in 2005, the show has enjoyed runs at the British National Railway Museum in York, London Waterloo and King's Cross Stations, and Toronto's Heritage Railway Museum in Canada. Purpose-built theatres surround a real rail track, and the show features one of the biggest guest stars ever to tread the boards: one of a number of original steam locomotives on loan from the British National Railway Museum.

Play/Musical: *The 39 Steps*
Year: 2005 onwards

This is the theatre production of the 1915 John Buchan novel, which had already enjoyed success as a film on three separate occasions. This time it is played for laughs, with only four actors playing a multitude of characters through the mechanism of quick-fire costume and accent changes. This becomes particularly frantic during the on-board train scenes, when comic timing to the rhythm of the train becomes everything.

A TRAGEDY OF ELEPHANTINE PROPORTIONS

Jumbo the African elephant was the first international superstar from the animal kingdom. Born in East Africa in 1860, he spent time in Germany and France before arriving at London Zoo in 1866 (having been swapped for a rhinoceros that had to trundle off to the Jardin des Plantes in Paris). Amidst public outcry in Britain, including angry letters to Queen Victoria, Jumbo was sold to Barnum's Circus in America in 1882, where Jumbomania really took off. When he was killed in a tragic railway accident in Canada in 1885 (he was hit by a freight train on a railway line next to the circus), his death was met with grief and sorrow around the world.

RAILWAY PRESERVATION AND ENTHUSIASM

It means more to me to be on the cover of Model Railroader *than to be on the cover of a music magazine.*

Rod Stewart

A lot of people spend a lot of time and effort preserving, modelling, travelling on, playing with or just enthusing about trains and railways. Many of them got the bug working on the railways for real, many have never shaken off the thrill of the first train set they received from Father Christmas, and many have needed a serious hobby to spend their cash on or fill their spare time with. They all have one thing in common: a love of trains and railways. This chapter is dedicated to those who preserve trains and railways that would otherwise be lost forever, those who painstakingly reproduce the real thing in miniature model form, those who collect the associated memorabilia and those who spend anything up to an entire lifetime spotting and recording whatever moves on two rails.

HERITAGE RAILWAYS

Railways generally need preserving by private groups when a government or national railway company has deemed them no longer profitable or worth funding, or after they have fallen into disrepair following the end of their useful working life. The vast majority of them become heritage railways, which is to say that they enjoy a new lease of life as a tourist attraction. Railway preservation is a costly business, no matter how many volunteers step forward to give up their time for the cause, so the income from tourism is vital to the survival of most preserved railways.

Such is the determination and enthusiasm of the people who do step forward to preserve this important part of their cultural history that there are now thousands of heritage railways dotted around more than 40 of the world's countries. Here is a very small sample to alert you to the bewildering array of choices on offer:

 **Name:** Bluebell Railway
Location: East and West Sussex, England
Original parent railway: London, Brighton and South Coast Railway
Type: standard gauge, steam
Length of track: 11 miles

The first preserved standard-gauge, steam-driven passenger service in the world, railways like this one allow us to relive the golden age of steam. A particular highlight is the Golden Arrow Pullman experience, a recreation of the glamorous London to Paris service once favoured by those who liked to fine-dine on the go. The railway has over 30 steam locomotives, around 150 carriages and wagons, and a station (Sheffield Park) that has been restored to its original

Victorian splendour. A film-maker's paradise, the railway's star appearances have included some classic British productions, including the 1985 film *A Room with a View*, the acclaimed period drama *Downton Abbey* and the final episode of revered sitcom *It Ain't Half Hot, Mum*.

Name: Strathspey Steam Railway
Location: Scottish Highlands
Original parent railway: Inverness and Perth Junction Railway
Type: standard gauge, steam and diesel
Length of track: 10 miles

This railway runs from the ski resort of Aviemore through Boat of Garten (famous for its osprey population) to Broomhill (the station known to millions of *Monarch of the Glen* viewers in Britain as 'Glenbogle'). If ospreys aren't your thing (really?), you could watch out instead for the family of oystercatchers (the little waders with the long bright-orange beaks) that nest every spring between the lines of the railway between Broomhill and Boat of Garten.

Although they have plenty of diesel back-up, most of the heritage runs are hauled by a majestic-looking LMS (London, Midland and Scottish Railway) Ivatt Class 2 2-6-0 steam locomotive.

Name: Giant's Causeway and Bushmills Railway
Location: Country Antrim, Northern Ireland
Original parent railway: Giant's Causeway, Portrush and Bush Valley Railway
Type: narrow gauge, steam and diesel
Length of track: 2 miles

It might be only 2 miles long, but at one end it has Northern Ireland's top tourist attraction, the Giant's Causeway, and at the other the home of one of the world's favourite tipples, the Bushmills Distillery. In between stations, you can admire sand dunes and a links golf course, both typical of this part of the country. This railway started life as the world's longest electric tramway but is now largely diesel-powered, with the odd 'steam special' being tugged along by one of their two small (0-4-0) tank engines.

Name: Snowdon Mountain Railway
Location: Gwynedd, Wales
Original parent railway: Snowdon Mountain Railway
Type: rack and pinion, steam and diesel
Length of track: 4.7 miles

Not too much can survive at a height of 1,085 metres above sea level, mostly just alpine flowers, mountain goats, waterfalls, low-flying clouds and, of course, train passengers. Yes, there is a railway station at the summit of Snowdon, the highest peak in England and Wales. The only public rack-and-pinion (think of a train running up and down a zip) railway in Britain, it has been a popular tourist attraction for over a hundred years. If you don't have a head for heights, stay and admire the lush green valleys below.

THE PLEASURE TRAIN

The longest pleasure pier in the world is at Southend-on-Sea in Essex, reaching 1.34 miles out into the Thames Estuary. That makes the diesel-powered, narrow-gauge Southend Pier Railway the longest pleasure-pier railway in the world, because its sole purpose is to carry passengers from shore to pier head and back again.

Name: North Borneo Railway
Location: Sabah, Malaysia
Original parent railway: North Borneo Railway

Type: standard gauge, steam
Length of track: 33 miles

Enjoy the sights, sounds and smells of local villages, temples, markets, mangrove swamps, paddy fields, rubber and coffee plantations, lush jungle and the South China Sea, all in a single journey. A British Vulcan 2-6-2 wood-burning steam locomotive pulls beautiful wooden carriages full of passengers doing that most colonial of things: having a piping-hot tiffin lunch while being cooled by the breeze offered by open windows and proper ceiling fans.

Name: Tequila Express
Location: Guadalajara, Mexico
Original parent railway: Ferrocarriles Nacionales de México

Type: standard gauge, diesel
Length of track: 25 miles

A train that runs through fields of blue agave (the base ingredient of tequila) from Guadalajara to the tequila distillery of San José del Refugio Hacienda. Tequila tastings and live mariachi music are provided on board, and dinner is served (with more tequila) at the hacienda. The scenery is worth seeing, but how much of it you remember the next day rather depends on your tequila intake.

Name: Froissy–Dompierre Light Railway
Location: Haute Somme, France
Type: narrow gauge, steam and diesel
Length of track: 4.3 miles

Also know as Le Petit Train de la Haute Somme, this railway is the last survivor of the narrow-gauge lines built to supply the British and French armies and their allies serving in the trench-filled battlefields of World War One. It has several operational steam and diesel locomotives running alongside the towpath of the River Somme and houses the Military and Industrial Railways Museum at the Froissy end.

Name: Sugar Cane Train
Location: Lahaina, Hawaii
Original parent railway: Lahaina, Kaanapali and Pacific Railroad
Type: narrow gauge, steam
Length of track: 6 miles

As its name suggests, the railway was originally built to haul sugar cane from plantation to mill. The highlight is a 100-metre curved wooden trestle bridge, from which passengers can see neighbouring

Hawaiian islands and the volcanic West Maui Mountains. Between December and April each year it is also not uncommon to spot humpback whales in the surrounding waters. The railway has one tender and two saddle-tank steam locomotives, one of which still sports its iconic cowcatcher.

BRANCHING OUT

Not all defunct branch lines have been lucky enough to be restored as operational railways, but some have at least achieved the next best thing following their conversion to walking, cycling and/or bridle paths. One such success story in England is the Cuckoo Line, a single-track service that once operated in Kent and East Sussex. Even though you can no longer enjoy them from a train, you can still take pleasure in the rural views that once delighted the Cuckoo Line's passengers.

PRESERVATION, PRESERVATION, PRESERVATION

Heritage railways are just one form of railway preservation around the world. Many countries also have one or more railway museums. Hundreds of skilled railway engineers continue to restore locomotives and carriages to their former glory so that they can be admired in those museums or, even better, travelled on along heritage lines. Whole railway stations have been restored with painstaking attention to detail, from old enamel advertising signs to Victorian station urinals to uniforms that recreate the look of some bygone age or other. From the restoration of the world's most famous train to a historically significant luggage van, here is a very brief flavour of what all these preservers are preserving for grateful generations to come.

Fairy Queen

EIR (East India Railways) 22 is the world's oldest preserved operating steam locomotive. Built in 1855 by Kitson and Company in Leeds, West Yorkshire, the 2-2-2 tank engine, which served as a troop carrier during the Indian Rebellion of 1857, now pulls a broad-gauge heritage service in India from

New Delhi to Alwar in Rajasthan, at a top speed of 25 mph. Its sibling locomotive, EIR 21, has recently been restored by India's Southern Railway and is now vying for the title of 'world's oldest', but as the two locomotives originally arrived in India in the same batch they might as well share the honour.

Furness Railway No. 20

The oldest preserved operational standard-gauge steam locomotive in Britain, known simply as FR 20, can often be seen at Locomotion, the National Railway Museum site at Shildon in County Durham. It is such a star, though, that it often doesn't get much rest between the guest appearances that it makes across the length and breadth of Britain. A 0-4-0 tender engine, it was originally built in 1863 by Sharp, Stewart and Company in Manchester.

Flying Scotsman

You know that railway preservers mean business when they embark on an overhaul that is going to last for ten years, but maybe they felt it was appropriate given the amount of effort and money that has been spent rescuing it from the scrapheap time and again, or maybe they just thought it was the least they could do for the most famous locomotive in the world. Either way, we and future generations owe them a debt. It is scarcely believable that something of that size and engineering complexity could be stripped back to its individual components and put back together again in a way that will allow it to run mainline rail tours in the twenty-first century.

British National Railway Museum

British rail heritage is vast, so vast that its national collection is spread over two sites, the main one being at York in North Yorkshire, the other at Shildon in County Durham. At York alone, there are over 100 locomotives and around 300 other items of rolling stock. A visit to the most-visited museum in Britain outside of London makes it very difficult not to feel the size and age of a small child as you wander among some of the most impressive locomotives ever built. If, like me, you are not unnecessarily tall, many of the locomotive wheels alone will be taller than you are.

The 'Mikados' of Japan

Although these Class D51 2-8-2 steam tender locomotives were retired in Japan as long ago as 1975, and only two or three have been restored to operational order, over 170 of them have nonetheless been preserved across the country. Powerful and majestic-looking, these black locomotives (known as *Degoichi* in Japanese) were so revered by Japanese rail enthusiasts that around 8,000 devotees attended a last-rites ceremony when the final ones were retired.

The railroad museums of North America

There are more than 300 railroad museums across the USA and Canada. Only three US and two Canadian states do not have one. Between them, they contain a truly huge number of steam and diesel locomotives and railroad carriages. That's a lot of preservation that's needed right there, one of the reasons that Railcamp is one of the summer-camp options open to American high-school students who might like to take messing around with trains to a serious level.

Passenger luggage van 132

One of the most significant preserved railway carriages can be found at the Kent and East Sussex Railway. It was used during its working life for three significant repatriations to the UK. In 1919 it brought home the remains of Edith Cavell, the nurse who had been executed for helping British POWs escape from occupied Belgium, and merchant seaman Captain Charles Fryatt, who had been captured and executed after ramming a German U-boat with his ferry while en route from Harwich to the Hook of Holland. When it was decided the following year that the remains of an unknown warrior were to be brought from France to lie amongst the kings and queens buried at Westminster Abbey, passenger luggage van 132 was the obvious choice for the job.

A miniature railway is no small engineering feat!

Miniature railways are scaled-down replicas of full-size ones, like the Romney, Hythe and Dymchurch Railway in Kent. Built in 1926 on a very narrow gauge of 38 centimetres, it was nonetheless built and operated as a public service (as opposed to a tourist service) and continues to provide local school and shopping runs to this day.

It is a one-third-scale representation of the London and North East Railway's mainline train service from London to Edinburgh as it was in the 1920s. The locomotives, therefore, included one-third replicas of Sir Nigel Gresley's famous A1 Pacifics. Indeed, Gresley himself was so impressed that he turned up in person at the grand opening in 1926. In another major PR coup, the railway somehow convinced Stan Laurel and Oliver Hardy to come along to the grand reopening in 1947 after World War Two. Stanley, at least, had no problem slipping into the scaled-down driver's cab for the publicity shots.

Cadeby Rectory Railway

Men of the cloth have long been drawn to the railways (the most famous example, of course, being the Reverend W. Awdry), and the Reverend Teddy Boston was no exception. He wanted to build a railway in the garden of his rectory in Cadeby in Leicestershire in the 1960s, but his garden wasn't very big and he couldn't afford to buy a scale replica that would fit into it, so he went ahead and bought a real, full-size steam engine instead! He purchased a W. G. Bagnall 0-4-0 saddle-tank locomotive from a nearby quarry, which also kindly donated two carriages and 98 metres of track, which was all the track the cleric ever had. The steam train ran up and down the short track until 2005, when it was dismantled and moved to the Moseley Railway Trust in Staffordshire, where it can still be seen.

Brand-new old trains

Perhaps the most impressive piece of rail preservation in recent years wasn't rail preservation at all. In 2008, against all the odds and in the face of many doubters, a brand-new Peppercorn Class A1 4-6-2 Pacific steam locomotive, numbered 60163 and named *Tornado*, was completed and made its maiden voyage from Darlington in County Durham to London King's Cross. It had taken 18 years and £3 million of donations to build, and it looked, sounded and performed like the real thing. That's because it is the real thing, and as such it continues to run mainline tours around Britain.

A second locomotive is now under construction, this time a P2 2-8-2 Mikado along the lines of the six originals of that Gresley class introduced between 1934 and 1936. The first of the six Mikado originals built in 1934 was the famous 2001 *Cock o' the North*; the new Mikado is to be known as 2007 *Prince of Wales*.

THE WORLD OF MODEL RAILWAYS

When English inventor Frank Hornby started to produce small-scale clockwork model trains in the 1920s, he could scarcely have envisaged that the Hornby name would be going strong almost a century later or that the world would now have over a hundred model railway manufacturers.

Clockwork has long since given way to state-of-the-art electric power, the latest incarnation of which is digital command control, which allows more than one train to be controlled on the same track at the same time. Manufacturers in different countries produce models to different scales, designed to run on different track gauges.

Size matters

The 00 scale is the standard in Britain, which means that each train model is built to 1/76 the size of the original 'real-life' train and that the track gauge required is a width between the rails of 16.5 mm. H0 (1/87) is the slightly different scale used in North America and continental Europe, and was so called because it started life as half the size of 0, the previous scale that German manufacturers had been building to since the start of the twentieth century. Japan uses the considerably smaller N scale (1/150), which means a lot of trimming for any Bonsai trees they might cultivate as part of the railway's scenery.

Bit by bit

It is needless to say, perhaps, that all other components of a model railway layout need to be built to the same scale as the trains and track. Stations, sheds, bridges, tunnels, railway employees, passengers, cows, sheep and everything else besides are made to an astonishing degree of accuracy with a quite bewildering variety of materials. If you're not a practical person, you can't build a model railway layout from scratch, but you can buy one, bit by bit, and millions of people around the world do just that.

Big business

The model railway business (or railroad modelling business, if you're reading this in North America) is a multibillion-pound industry running alongside a thriving second-hand market, with original pieces from the 1950s and 1960s going for vast sums of money. Clubs and societies span the globe, as do the manufacturers, dealers and magazine publishers required to feed the hunger for all things related to railway modelling.

Miniatur Wunderland

Located in Hamburg, Germany, this model railway consists of 8 miles of H0-scale track, about a thousand trains consisting of around 12,000 carriages, 400,000 lights, 250,000 trees and about the same amount of human figurines. If you look very closely, you might even see a small-scale Michael Portillo, which he painted himself when he visited the exhibition during the filming of *Great Continental Railway Journeys* for the BBC. The layout has many different sections, including those set in Germany, Austria, Scandinavia and the US. Planned additions include sections representing Italy, France, England and parts of Africa. The Braun twins, Gerrit and Frederik, and their 270 employees have been building it up since 2000.

Celebrity railway enthusiasts

If you think that railway enthusiasts generally live at home in the relative obscurity of their loft conversions, away from the outside world and rarely seeing daylight, you might reconsider when you have read the following list of rather well-known celebrities who have found time to indulge in a train-related hobby while doing some other stuff with their lives as well:

➤ **Pete Waterman:** As a member of the Stock, Aitken & Waterman hit factory, English record producer Waterman made enough money to indulge his real passion: trains. He pretty much spent his childhood spotting trains on Leamington Spa Station, a complex model of which he has been building at his home for several years. He also owns a number of real steam and diesel locomotives in various states of repair and renovation, and he even did some work on the Flying Scotsman during the time he was part-owner of the train.

➤ **Rod Stewart:** Well known for his rock music and his footballing obsession, but less so as a railway modeller. The layouts in his Beverley Hills mansion, which have featured in three separate issues of *Model Railroader* magazine, include a 1/87 (H0-scale) model of New York's Grand Central Station, which the British singer-songwriter built bit by bit while on the road touring.

➤ **Frank Sinatra:** At his home in Rancho Mirage, California, Ol' Blue Eyes had an entire 'train cottage' full of Lionel and American Flyer models (Lionel was the US equivalent of Hornby in Britain and ended up merging with American Flyer, just as Hornby ended up merging with Tri-ang in Britain). His collection was sold with the ranch after his death and is valued at over $1 million.

➤ **Hermann Göring:** The Luftwaffe commander had two train sets covering 400 square metres in his country home north of Berlin and was often photographed showing them off to visiting dignitaries, including Adolf Hitler. They were typical of the 0-gauge tinplate trains and track made by German toy company Märklin in the 1930s, but Göring had one of the layouts modified with an overhead aeroplane system that allowed him to drop little wooden bombs onto the trains below. This just may have been what convinced Hitler to appoint him Commander-in-Chief of the Luftwaffe in 1935.

➤ **Johnny Cash:** A train collector who sang lots of country songs about the American railroad (including 'I've Got a Thing About Trains'!) and starred in singing TV commercials for his favourite Lionel trains in the 1970s.

➤ **Tim Berners-Lee:** The English scientist started trainspotting when he attended a London school that sat between two railway tracks. Because he was no good at sport, he also stayed in his room and played with his train set a lot. He made some electronic gadgets to better control his trains, became interested in electronics per se as a direct result of having done so, and went on to invent the World

Wide Web. Without train sets, there would be no Internet. That's all I'm saying.

Trainspotting

The decline of trainspotting coincided with the decline of steam from the 1960s onwards, because multiple diesel or electrical units were never going to be as sexy as wooden Pullman carriages rattling through stations behind a screaming steam locomotive, especially if the locomotive in question was 'famous', like *Mallard* or *Flying Scotsman*. But trainspotters do still exist, even if they now find themselves on the endangered species list.

They were always considered a subspecies of the human race by the chattering classes in any event. Even now, the Oxford English Dictionary is somewhat dismissive in its treatment of them, describing a trainspotter as 'a person who collects locomotive numbers as a hobby'. This makes the assumption that the simple trainspotter cannot possibly be interested in the mechanics or look or history of a train, only in its number. Maybe that is indeed true in some cases, but at least the simple souls are out there getting some fresh air.

Perhaps trainspotting might make a comeback in the twenty-first century, though, if high-speed-train advertising takes off in a big way. Known as 'carriage wrapping', examples on Britain's railways already include a whole East Coast Main Line train covered with the branding of the 007 film *Skyfall*, and entire Virgin trains promoting *Superman Returns* and *X-Men, Days of Future Past*. If you've got your book handy, the East Coast Main Line Class 91 locomotive that pulled *Skyfall* was renumbered 91 007 (see what they did there?) for the duration of the advertising campaign. Tick.

STATION ETIQUETTE

People who find it necessary to vomit whilst in a railway carriage should discreetly use their hats; this would come naturally to anyone properly brought up.

From a letter to *Picture Post* magazine, 1952

Gentlemen, please adjust your dress before leaving

Notice placed at the exit of British railway station toilets in the last century (I think it meant something different then!)

FULL STEAM AHEAD

*Anything is possible on a train:
a great meal, a binge... an
intrigue, a great night's sleep.*

Paul Theroux

As the twenty-first century races ahead, it seems certain that trains and railways will continue to enjoy something of a revival around the world. Those who care even a bit for the environment (it has been estimated that one car consumes half the energy of an entire high-speed train), or who don't much like sitting in traffic on increasingly congested roads, or who don't like airport queues and security checks, can see the obvious benefits of improved rail travel.

For those who need to get around the cities of the world, comfortable, efficient urban railways above or below ground continue to grow. For those who need to get from one city to another quickly, more high-speed links are proposed, planned or underway on every continent of the world that isn't covered in snow and ice. It has even been suggested that maglev trains could reach 500 mph by the year 2020 – they can get up to 340 mph now.

In continental western Europe and Japan, it remains largely the case that high-speed train beats plane for time, and often on cost, over distances of up to 500 miles. In Japan the car is increasingly being dismissed as an expensive, inefficient and environmentally unfriendly plaything when compared to the clean, superfast, efficient bullet trains on offer.

Britain once led the way and gave railways to the world before short-sighted politicians and self-serving businessmen in the second half of the twenty-first century undid much of the earlier good work. But we appear to have turned the tide, with significant ongoing investment in high-speed trains, network electrification and, to some extent, biofuels. The Crossrail project is the largest construction project in Europe and will increase capacity and reduce journey times across London by 2018, and the proposed High Speed 2 project will offer high-speed services from London to Birmingham, Manchester and Leeds. Britain's railways are already busier than at any time since the 1920s and are set to get a lot busier still.

It is perhaps a dichotomy of our times that we crave the benefits of modern train travel alongside our nostalgia for the golden ages of steam and vintage diesel. Thanks to the efforts of the many volunteers around the world who work tirelessly to preserve the locomotives and railway lines of old, we can have both. But the real thrill will always be the first time we travel on a particular train or line, however old or new it might be, especially when we do so in a different country or travel to a destination that is new to us.

Travelling by train is not just about the journey, but it's not just about the destination either. It's about both, and long may that continue to be so.